W9-CBN-291

A CELEBRATION OF
IRELAND

A CELEBRATION OF
IRELAND

Janice Anderson

Gill & Macmillan

PAGES 2-3: The Gap of Dunloe with Macgillycuddy's Reeks reaching skywards, near Killarney, Co. Kerry.

THESE PAGES: A typical Connemara cottage, near Recess, Co. Galway.

ACKNOWLEDGEMENTS
All pictures in this book are reproduced by kind permission of © Don Sutton International Picture Library, Dublin with the exception of the map on page 6 which is by Julian Baker Illustrations; the detail from the Book of Kells on page 13 which is reproduced by kind permission of Trinity College, Dublin; the portrait of Oscar Wilde on page 16 © Range Pictures/Bettman Archive; the portrait of George Bernard Shaw on page 17 © Hulton Deutsch Collection Ltd.; the photograph of U2 on page 45 by Brendan Beirne © Rex Features London; the photograph of Sinéad O'Connor by P. H. Woody © Rex Features London; and the portrait of William Butler Yeats on page 70 © Hulton Deutsch Collection Ltd.

Published in Ireland by
Gill & Macmillan Ltd
Hume Avenue
Park West
Dublin 12
with associated companies throughout the world.
www.gillmacmillan.ie

Copyright © 1998, 2001 Regency House Publishing Limited
3 Mill Lane, Broxbourne, Hertfordshire, EN10 7AZ, UK.

ISBN 0 7171 2680 3

All rights reserved. No part of this book may be reproduced in any form or by any electronic or mechanical means including information, storage and retrieval systems, without permission in writing from the publisher.

A catalogue record for this book is available from the British Library

Printed in India

Contents

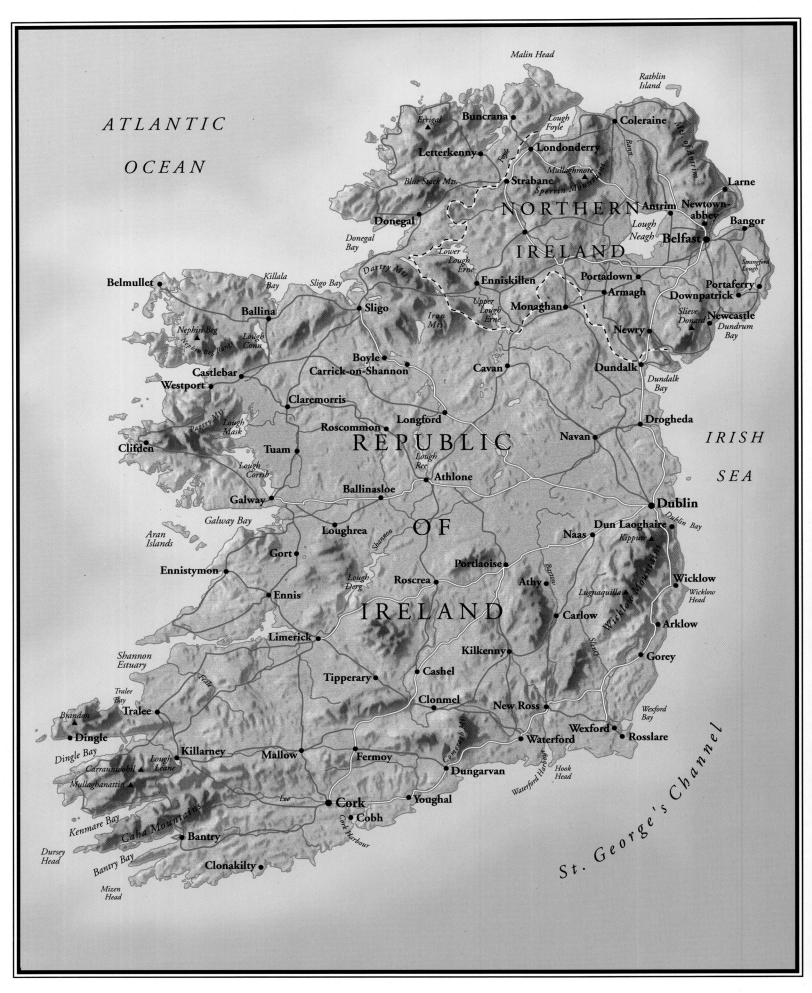

ATLANTIC

OCEAN

Malin Head

Rathlin Island

Errigal ▲ Buncrana ●
Lough Foyle
Coleraine ●

Letterkenny ● Londonderry ●

Mullaghmore ▲ Larne ●

Blue Stack Mts. Strabane ● Sperrin Mountains Antrim ● Newtown-abbey ●

NORTHERN Bangor ●

Donegal ● Lough Neagh Belfast ●

Donegal Bay IRELAND Strangford Lough

Dartry Mts. Lower Lough Erne Portadown ● Portaferry ●

Belmullet ● Killala Bay Sligo Bay Enniskillen ● Armagh ● Downpatrick ●

Ballina ● Upper Lough Erne Monaghan ● Slieve Donard ▲ Newcastle ●

Nephin Beg ▲ Sligo ● Iron Mts. Newry ● Dundrum Bay

Lough Conn Boyle ● Cavan ● Dundalk ●

Castlebar ● Carrick-on-Shannon ● Dundalk Bay

Westport ● Claremorris ● Longford ● Drogheda ●

Clifden ● Lough Mask Roscommon ● Navan ● IRISH

REPUBLIC SEA

Tuam ● Lough Ree

Lough Corrib Athlone ●

Galway ● Ballinasloe ● Dublin ●

Galway Bay Loughrea ● OF Dun Laoghaire ● Dublin Bay

Aran Islands Naas ● Kippure ▲

Gort ● Shannon Portlaoise ● Wicklow ●

Ennistymon ● Lough Derg Roscrea ● Athy ● Lugnaquilla ▲ Wicklow Head

Ennis ● IRELAND Carlow ● Arklow ●

Limerick ● Kilkenny ● Gorey ●

Shannon Estuary Tipperary ● Cashel ●

Tralee Bay Feale Clonmel ● New Ross ● Wexford Bay

Brandon ▲ Tralee ● Waterford ● Wexford ●

Dingle ● Killarney ● Mallow ● Fermoy ● Comeragh Mts. Rosslare ●

Dingle Bay Lough Leane Dungarvan ● Hook Head

Carrauntoohil ▲ Lee Cork ● Youghal ● Waterford Harbour

Mullaghanattin ▲ Cobh ●

Kenmare Bay Caha Mountains Cork Harbour

Dursey Head Bantry ●

Bantry Bay Clonakilty ●

Mizen Head

St. George's Channel

6

Introduction

'A Hundred Thousand Welcomes – *Céad Míle Fáilte'* is how they greet you all over Ireland. It is a neat summing up of everything the visitor has come to expect of the country: a warmly relaxed welcome from a friendly people, famed for their way with words and possessed of more than a touch of the romantically exotic, inherited from the Gaels (Celts), who were the first to bring true civilization and a rich culture to the island.

Ireland lies on the western edge of the great European land mass, its eastern edge tucked into the largest island of Great Britain, its western coast thrusting out into the Atlantic Ocean. It is not a very big island – just over 480km (300 miles) from top to bottom and about 275km (170 miles) at its widest point.

It is an island with few natural resources: no oil, some coal in Tipperary, Europe's largest lead and zinc mine in County Meath, and large stretches of peat bog, still an important source of natural fuel, which itself was the result of the unchecked felling of primeval forest which, by about 1700, left Ireland the most sparsely wooded country in Europe. But Ireland is also one of the loveliest and most appealing of Europe's islands, with a mild climate because of the Gulf Stream and a high rainfall, particularly in the west which faces into the Atlantic. The rainfall accounts for the glorious green of much of the country: there is good reason for Ireland to be called 'the Emerald Isle'.

Despite the fact that the larger of the two states sharing the island, the Republic of Ireland,

is one of the boom economies of the European Union, with a success built on fast-growing industries, Ireland is still very much a rural country, a haven of tranquillity far from the bustle of late-20th-century city life.

A main reason for the island's predominantly rural aspect is that it is generally underpopulated. In a land where the population was already greatly reduced by two centuries of emigration, caused in part by choice and in part by grim necessity, there has also been a move away from the countryside and into the towns and cities. More than a third of the Republic's population, which is small by European standards, lives in or around Dublin, while Belfast, the largest city in Northern Ireland, also has by far the largest concentration, with almost a quarter of the Province's total population.

The Ireland of the imagination, the quiet land of fields and thatched cottages, still manages to surprise visitors with the great variety of its contrasting scenery. True, there are the green valleys watered by great rivers and pretty streams, like something out of a Hollywood movie, but there are also the wild places, the limestone country of The Burren and the Aran islands, the strange basalt rock formations of the Giant's Causeway on north Antrim's dramatic coast, and the wind-swept remoteness of much of the mountain country to the west, where belief in the 'little people' of Celtic myth has survived longest and where the majority of people still speak the Irish language.

Water, in thousands of lakes and hundreds of rivers, streams and waterways, gives the

countryside a softly shining beauty, unique to Ireland and adds greatly to its attraction as a place where one can take a holiday and get away from it all. It is possible to pass quiet hours completely undisturbed while fishing in rivers and lakes teeming with fish, or watching the birdlife that congregates in great numbers along their banks and shores.

If the faster pace of town and city life is something you can't altogether do without, then Ireland can offer that, too, in splendid variety, from the mixture of Georgian elegance, modern style and bohemian life, which is Dublin at the end of the century, to the medieval maze with more than a touch of the modern which characterizes towns like Kilkenny, Galway and Waterford.

Belfast, too, plagued by the Troubles which have dominated life in Northern Ireland for so long and which are themselves the terrible legacy of centuries of bitter strife and tragedy throughout the island, still retains its heart and a solid core of Victorian solidity and the city's new Waterfront Hall, a splendidly Modernist, predominantly glass concert hall built on the banks of the River Lagan, is seen by many as an optimistic, hopeful look into a happier future.

Doonagore Castle, set inside its small bawn, *or walled enclosure, overlooks the Atlantic near the village of Doolin on the Cliffs of Moher coast in Co. Clare.*

Chapter One
Dublin

Dublin, in the Republic of Ireland, is one of the fastest-growing capital cities in Europe. Because it is also a gracious city and a compact one, offering many attractions within walking distance of one another, it is also one of Europe's most popular tourist destinations.

Dublin has grown fast in recent decades, its suburbs overspilling into the surrounding County Dublin. It is the largest urban area in Ireland and home to a third of the Republic's total population, forcing it to confront many of the problems of 20th-century urban living, including inner-city deprivation and drug abuse. But even if Dublin appears to share many of the positive, as well as negative, characteristics of any great city, it undoubtedly has an atmosphere of energy and dynamism, born no doubt of the inevitable spin-off between traditional conservatism and youthful, cosmopolitan get-up-and-go, that make it uniquely attractive among the great cities of the world.

Today's Dublin could, at first glance, be seen as typical of any modern city, full of discos and clubs, cafés, restaurants, and boutiques (providing the designer labels so essential to today's international consumer society), and a good sprinkling of estate agent's boards, evidence of a boom in the property market; but it exists on the foundation of a centuries-long history still evident in many parts of the modern city.

Dublin, the heart and mainspring of County Dublin, is superbly situated on Dublin Bay at the mouth of the River Liffey and with the Wicklow Mountains making a fine backdrop to the south. It is a setting that has attracted people since prehistoric times, and a map by the second-century astronomer and geographer, Ptolemy, clearly shows a settlement called Eblana established on the Liffey.

Celts versus Vikings

St. Patrick may have come here in the mid-fifth century, and the Norwegian Vikings, descending on the British Isles from their sub-arctic homes, certainly did some 400 years later. Around A.D. 840 they ousted the Celts who were living here and established a trading settlement of their own on the south bank of the Liffey.

The Viking's name for their riverside settlement derived from the Celtic words for 'Dark Pool' – *Dubh Linn* – and this name has endured, although the name for the Celtic settlement on the north bank of the Liffey with which Dublin eventually merged, *Baile Atha Cliath*, meaning 'town of the hurdle ford', is the Irish name for Dublin to this day. The Viking hold on Dublin lasted until the mighty Irish warrior king, Brian Boru, defeated them at the Battle of Clontarf in 1014.

In the 12th century, the Anglo-Normans in England turned covetous eyes towards Ireland. A call for help from one of the several kings then ruling Ireland, who had been turned off his throne

ABOVE
Looking west up the River Liffey: a view dominated by several of the 14 bridges which cross the river in the city of Dublin.

OPPOSITE
Nestling behind an archway off Lower Bridge Street, the Brazen Head is said to be the oldest bar in Dublin, and even in the whole of Ireland; there has been an inn on the site since the end of the 12th century, though the present building dates from the 17th century.

increasingly important roles in the life of the city and of Ireland beyond.

By this time, the British viceroy had moved out of Dublin Castle and taken up court in a grand residence in Phoenix Park, to the west of the city and one of the largest urban parks in Europe. When the Irish Free State, later the Republic, came into being, Dublin was naturally its capital and its heart; the viceroy's residence became the official residence of the President of Ireland.

The infamous Kilmainham Jail, also in the western suburbs of Dublin, south of Phoenix Park and the Liffey was opened in 1795 and used to house many political prisoners, including Charles Stewart Parnell and Eamon de Valera. It is now empty, preserved as a grim museum and symbol of the struggle for Irish independence.

Historic Dublin in Today's City

The early history of Dublin, when Viking and Celtic settlements were established on either side of the Liffey, still shows in the present-day city, spreading away from both banks of the river, which is spanned by a fine collection of bridges, including the splendid O'Connell Bridge. Pause in the centre of it and look downstream when you will see one of the finest views of Dublin, including the span of the delicately slender Ha'penny Bridge.

The city north of the Liffey, bisected by the wide ribbon of O'Connell Street, named after the 'Liberator', Daniel O'Connell, is where the louder, more down-to-earth and, sometimes, more raucous aspects of Dublin life are apparent. The historic General Post Office, at the centre of the Easter Rising of 1916, and the Abbey Theatre, the country's National Theatre, are both in this area, as is the Dublin Writers' Museum, housed in

by a neighbouring ruler, was too good an opportunity to miss. In 1170, the first of the Plantagenet kings of England, Henry II, sent in a force of Welsh knights led by Richard de Clare, known as Strongbow, to help the ex-king of Leinster, who, in turn, swore an oath of fealty to Henry. Strongbow established himself in Ireland, rather too strongly for Henry's liking, and the king set up his own court in Dublin, extending his rule over most of Leinster. From then on, until the 20th century, Dublin was the main base for English influence in Ireland, firmly at the heart of both political and social life.

The small town began to expand in the 17th

century, reaching its heyday in the next century. This was when the building of what is still called Georgian Dublin began, along with the establishment of Dublin as a major centre of brewing, Arthur Guinness founding his famous brewery at St. James's Gate on the Liffey in 1759.

With the conceding of autonomy to the Irish parliament in 1783, Dublin blossomed into a centre of fashionable society, only to see it wane after the Irish Uprising of 1798 caused William Pitt to push through the reunion of the British and Irish parliaments in 1801. By the end of the 19th century, Dublin was very much a quiet Irish town, with strongly Irish cultural movements playing

two Georgian buildings in Parnell Square. The square, named after Charles Stewart Parnell, one of the heroes of the Irish independence movement, was originally called Rutland Square and was one of the first Georgian squares to be built in Dublin.

On the south bank of the river is most of what remains of Dublin's 18th-century heyday, when all that was most cultured and most fashionable in Ireland was centred round Dublin Castle, Trinity College, Leinster House and the gracious Georgian streets and squares, including the splendid St. Stephen's Green, where the houses of the well-heeled were to be found. Some of the more historic of Dublin's 800 pubs are on the south side of the Liffey, too, including Davy Byrne's in Duke Street, off Grafton Street. Here, in James Joyce's *Ulysses*, Leopold Bloom stopped for a sandwich and a glass of burgundy – an event still celebrated in Dublin every Bloomsday (16 June).

Both Leopold Bloom and his creator would be astonished if they could see Grafton Street today, for it has been pedestrianized and has quite a Continental air to it. It is one of Dublin's most fashionable streets, full of shops, department stores and cafés. Its attractions are many, including lively street entertainers, the oldest of the several Bewley's Oriental Cafés which are such an attractive part of Dublin's social life, and a splendid bronze statue of Molly Malone, heroine

OPPOSITE TOP LEFT
Leinster House, built for the Duke of Leinster on the south bank of the Liffey in Dublin in 1745. Since 1924, both houses of the Irish Parliament, the Dáil (the lower house) and the Seanad (the upper house), have met here.

OPPOSITE BELOW
St. Patrick's Cathedral, near Dublin Castle, is the national cathedral of the Church of Ireland. It is said to have been built over a place where Saint Patrick baptized converts to Christianity in the fifth century. The cathedral dates back to the 12th century.

LEFT
Another relic of Dublin's 18th-century heyday, the magnificent Custom House, built between 1781 and 1791, stretches along the north bank of the Liffey in the heart of Dublin.

BELOW
Popularly called the Ha'penny Bridge because of the toll that was levied on it until 1919, the Wellington Bridge, a footbridge over the Liffey in Dublin, was built in 1816, the year after the Irish-born Duke of Wellington's victory over Napoleon at Waterloo.

of the popular song, standing by her wheelbarrow of 'cockles and mussels, alive, alive-o'.

West of Grafton Street and still on the south, or right, bank of the Liffey, the area known as Temple Bar has become Dublin's answer to Paris' Left Bank. Here is where you will find small experimental theatres, second-hand bookshops, many art galleries and numerous bistros. Development of the area began in a small way, with people taking over disused warehouses; it was all rather shabby and run-down, having once been an area of craftsmen and artisans until creeping industrialization led to their demise. In recent years it has been gentrified in vaguely 18th-century style, with cobbled streets and old-fashioned street lighting.

Because, as elsewhere in the British Isles, most buildings in Ireland (especially domestic housing before the 17th century) were made of wood or wattle and daub, there is, in fact, very little of the early history of Dublin to be seen in the modern city and insensitive town planning which began in the 1960s did little to help: an extensive Viking site on Wood Quay, near Christ Church Cathedral, eventually disappeared, before it could be fully excavated, under some unattractive civic building in the 1980s.

Three buildings, all south of the Liffey, which can trace their origins back at least to the 12th century, are Dublin Castle and the two cathedrals, St. Patrick's and Christ Church, the Cathedral of the Holy Trinity.

Only the Record Tower, which served as the administration centre for British rule in Ireland between the 18th and 20th centuries remains of the original Dublin Castle, built in the first half of the 12th century over the 'dark pool' which gives Dublin its name. Most of the Dublin Castle you see today was built and rebuilt over the centuries, though there remains much of interest to visitors. The State Apartments include St. Patrick's Hall, where the Presidents of the Republic are inaugurated; the Wedgwood Room, decorated in the familiar blue-and-white style of Wedgwood china; and the Throne Room, dominated by a huge throne and last used by Elizabeth II's grandfather, George V.

Christ Church is the older of Dublin's two cathedrals, having been founded by a Norse king, Sitric, in 1038. Its magnificent Gothic crypt, crossings and transepts date from two centuries later. The remains of Strongbow, who died in 1176, and what is possibly his monument, can be seen in the cathedral, and – a delightfully Irish touch – a cat in pursuit of a rat who were discovered last century, stuck in the organ pipes:

their 'tomb' is a glass case in which their mummified bodies are displayed.

St. Patrick's Cathedral, just south of Dublin Castle, was founded in 1190 on the legendary site of baptisms carried out by St. Patrick in the fifth century. The present building dates back to 1225, though it has been much altered, rebuilt and enlarged since then. The tomb that most interests visitors here is that of Jonathan Swift, author of *Gulliver's Travels* and many other satirical writings, who was Dean of St. Patrick's between 1713 and 1745. The pulpit from which he regularly preached is still preserved in the cathedral, though it is no longer used.

Ireland's Heritage Preserved

In the area of Dublin south of the Liffey, from the castle and cathedrals eastwards, are to be found many of the buildings most intimately connected with Ireland's history and culture.

When the immensely rich Duke of Leinster built his town house, Leinster House, in green fields south of the Liffey rather than on the more fashionable north side in 1745, many people considered his action ill-judged. 'Not so,' said the duke, knowing full well that where he went, others would follow. Soon, the green fields were full of fine Georgian houses. Today, Leinster House is a

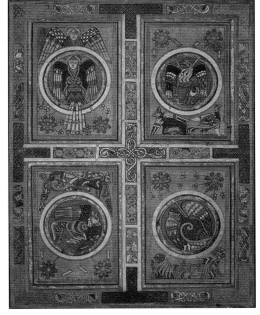

very important building in Dublin, for it houses the Dáil, Ireland's parliament. Two great rotundas, added at either side of Leinster House in 1890, now house the entrances to Ireland's National Library and National Museum.

Among the treasures of Irish history in the National Museum are the many artefacts found on the Viking site at Wood Quay, from combs and brooches to swords and weighing machines. The superb Tara Brooch and Ardagh Chalice, both dating from the eighth century, are in the museum's medieval collection, and there are other fine collections, imaginatively displayed, of Irish glass, lace and musical instruments.

A short walk from the Museum is the National Gallery of Ireland, opened in 1864 and housing a comprehensive collection of paintings and sculpture, covering most of the schools of European art; the gallery is also strong on Irish painting, including the work of Jack B. Yeats, brother of William Butler Yeats, and one of Ireland's best-known painters.

The National Library is of interest both for its fine collections of first editions and the works of Irish writers, and for the fact that James Joyce set Stephen Dedalus' literary debate in *Ulysses* in the library's Reading Room. However, to find the most famous books in Ireland, the *Book of Durrow* and the *Book of Kells*, you must go to the library of Trinity College.

Trinity College, set in 40 secluded acres in the centre of Dublin, was founded by Elizabeth I in 1591 and is the only college of Dublin University. The Long Room of the Old Library of Trinity College houses some 200,000 of the college's collection of over 3 million volumes, including the *Book of Kells*, a four-volume, superbly illuminated version of the Four Gospels. Two of the four volumes are usually on display in the library at any one time.

ABOVE
The Four Courts, completed in 1802 on a fine site on the north bank of the Liffey, houses four courts of justice, Common Pleas, Chancery, Exchequer and King's Bench. The superb building, its Corinthian portico crowned by figures of Justice and Mercy, among others, was carefully restored after being severely damaged during the Irish Civil War.

OPPOSITE
Downstream from the Ha'penny Bridge, O'Connell Bridge leads over the Liffey to O'Connell Street, the main thoroughfare of Dublin's Northside. The monument dominating

O'Connell Street is to Daniel O'Connell, the 'Liberator', whose life's work included the gaining of Catholic emancipation in Ireland and the search for Irish independence by peaceful means.

TOP
Trinity College's lawns and quadrangles offer havens of tranquillity at the heart of Dublin.

ABOVE
The Book of Kells, the richly decorated medieval manuscript which is one of the great treasures of the library of Trinity College.

Away From the Centre

Dublin has a fast and efficient commuter train service, called the DART (short for Dublin Area Rapid Transport), running round Dublin Bay, and linking Howth to the north of the city with Bray, beyond Dún Laoghaire, to the south in County Wicklow.

South of suburban coastal Dublin is the area which has been called the Dubliners' playground. There are attractive seaside villages such as Blackrock, Sandycove, Dalkey (which can boast two castles, two harbours and a cottage in which George Bernard Shaw once lived), and Killiney with its superb views across to Dalkey Island. Inland are the Dublin Mountains, with their forest walks and scenic drives, and other attractions like the race course at Leopardstown and the 16-hectare (40-acre) Fernhill Gardens south of Sandyford.

Dún Laoghaire, on the southern curve of Dublin Bay 14km (9 miles) south of Dublin, is both a major ferry terminal and the largest yachting centre in Ireland. The harbour, which has two mile-long piers, was built by the Scottish engineer, John Rennie, early in the 19th century. A short distance along the coast from Dún Laoghaire's harbour is Sandycove, a tiny village whose Martello Tower accommodated James Joyce for a week in 1904, and on which the author bestowed literary immortality by setting the opening of *Ulysses* there. There is now a James Joyce Museum in the Martello Tower, open in the summer months.

Like Dublin city centre, Sandycove also celebrates Bloomsday on 16 June – the day in 1904 when all the events in *Ulysses* took place. For Joyce, Sandycove was as much a part of Dublin as the more famous streets and buildings in the centre of the city; when he said that after his death, the word 'Dublin' would be found inscribed on his heart, he had the whole splendid spread of the city and its suburbs in his mind's eye.

OPPOSITE
An aerial view of Dalkey Island, lying a little way offshore from the attractive seaside town of Dalkey, south of Dublin. As well as a bird sanctuary, Dalkey Island boasts a Martello Tower and Saint Begnet's Holy Well, reputed to cure rheumatism.

BELOW
Sandycove, at the southern end of Dublin Bay, is renowned for its connections with James Joyce. Its Martello Tower, setting for the opening pages of Ulysses, *now houses a museum dedicated to the writer's life and work. The Forty Foot Pool, below the Tower, also figures in the novel's early pages.*

Irish Literature

Irish writers have added enormously to the body of literature written in English. Drama, poetry and fiction would be much the poorer but for the sparkling wit, rich vein of fantasy and elegant satire executed in those particular rhythms, derived from Gaelic speech patterns and the Gaelic literary tradition, which are unique to them. Ulster-born poet Seamus Heaney's Nobel Prize for Literature in 1995 was the fourth to be awarded to an Irish writer, the other three going to W. B. Yeats (1923), George Bernard Shaw (1925) and Samuel Beckett (1969).

At only a slightly less exalted level, writers from both the north and south of Ireland have figured prominently in the lists of winners and short-listed writers for the United Kingdom's Booker Prize for Fiction, among them Iris Murdoch (Dublin-born of Anglo-Irish parents),

Roddy Doyle, Molly Keane and Brian Moore. Molly Keane, following in the footsteps of Sheridan, Goldsmith, Wilde and Shaw, achieved early success in Britain as a playwright (using the name M. J. Farrell to conceal her identity, since well-brought-up Anglo-Irish girls did not write plays, let alone have them performed on the West End stage); by the time, many years later, that she began writing her brilliant and witty novels of life in the Anglo-Irish Big House, treading a path explored earlier in the century by Elizabeth Bowen, attitudes had radically changed and she was able to use her own name.

It was in the 17th century that many Irish writers began working in the English language rather than in Gaelic, which had been the language of the old Irish aristocracy, now deprived of power and patronage. Now the Protestant

Anglo-Irish were the ones wanting to read poetry and stories and see new plays at the theatre, and they required them to be in English.

Even a satirist like Jonathan Swift, born in Dublin of English parents in 1667, and aiming his barbs in political satires, including *Gulliver's Travels*, at the Anglo-Irish, knew that those same Anglo-Irish would be a large part of his audience. Swift went on to become Dean of St. Patrick's Cathedral in Dublin, where he is buried and where several items of memorabilia associated with his name attract many visitors.

A fellow student of Swift's at Trinity College, Dublin, was William Congreve; a few years after them, George Farquhar also studied at Trinity, the latter two becoming leading playwrights of their day – in England.

In fact, until well into the 20th century, most

ABOVE
Oscar Wilde, photographed in New York in 1882, when he was known as a poet and the 'apostle of aesthetics'; the novel Dorian Gray *and the plays including* Lady Windermere's Fan, An Ideal Husband *and* The Importance of Being Earnest *which would give him lasting fame were not published until the 1890s.*

RIGHT
Celebrating 'Bloomsday', 16 June, has become part of the summer season in Dublin. This stylishly dressed couple stand beside the statue of James Joyce sculpted by Marjorie Fitzgibbon, in North Earl Street in Dublin.

Irish writers wishing to achieve fame and fortune, or merely a modest living, had to leave Ireland to do so. After Congreve and Farquhar, the next Irish writers to set the London stage alight in the 18th century were Sheridan and Goldsmith. Late in the 19th century, the names had changed, but the Irish talent was still very much in evidence with such luminaries as essayist George Moore, and playwrights Dion Boucicault, Oscar Wilde and George Bernard Shaw.

By now, the Irish Revival, influenced by the Gaelic Revival at the end of the 19th century had been gathering pace. The Abbey Theatre, backed by W. B. Yeats and Lady Gregory, produced its first play in 1904. Its subject, and that of the many plays which followed, including works by great writers like J. M. Synge and Sean O'Casey, was Ireland, Irish life and Irish history. They were not always well-received by Irish audiences quick to see immorality in word as well as in deed: the first night of Synge's masterpiece, *The Playboy of the Western World*, turned into a riot because of its 'immoral language'.

While the Irish Revival meant that, from now on, many Irish writers, novelists and short story writers, poets and dramatists would find as interested a market for their work at home as

abroad, others, most notably James Joyce and Samuel Beckett, were forced to flee the narrowness of Irish society and seek sympathetic publishers abroad.

James Joyce, in particular, keenly felt the bitterness of exile from his beloved Dublin, the setting of his great works of fiction, including *Dubliners*, *Portrait of the Artist as A Young Man* and *Ulysses*. It was not until the 1960s that *Ulysses*, till then perceived as pornographic, was taken off the Republic of Ireland's lengthy list of banned works. Today, Bloomsday, named after Leopold Bloom, a main character in *Ulysses* and celebrated on 16 June, the day on which the events of the novel take place, is a highlight of the summer season in and around Dublin.

ABOVE
George Bernard Shaw at 70, by which time he had become the Grand Old Man of Anglo-Irish literature. Born into an Irish Protestant family in Dublin in 1856, Shaw did most of his writing in England, where he discovered the Socialism which became the inspiration and driving force behind his great plays and other writings.

LEFT
One of Patrick Kavanagh's poems was called 'Lines written on a seat on the Grand Canal', so a seat beside the Grand Canal in Dublin seemed the ideal place for a statue of the poet, who died in 1967.

Chapter Two
Around Dublin: The Eastern Counties –
Louth, Meath, Dublin, and Kildare

The eastern counties of the Republic of Ireland – Louth, Meath, Kildare and Wicklow which enclose Dublin in a crescent touching the Irish Sea coast to north and south – offer a splendid variety of scenery, from the quiet green pastures of Meath and Louth touching the Border with Northern Ireland in the north, to the rugged Wicklow Mountains in the south. Today, much of the region is fertile pastureland, though Kildare encompasses the Bog of Allen, the largest bogland area in Ireland, as well as the grassy plain of the Curragh, Ireland's largest area of arable land and centre of the country's thoroughbred racing industry.

Louth, a Border county, and Meath, both of them once within the Pale, which was the boundary within which the Crown had established total authority by about 1500, are areas of quiet farmland these days, attracting fewer holidaymakers and tourists than Wicklow or Kildare, also once within the Pale, despite the fine stretch of coast and numerous pleasant seaside resorts like Black Rock on Dundalk Bay and Bettystown, south of Drogheda.

County Meath, once part of an ancient province of Ireland ruled by the High Kings of Ireland from their palace crowning the Hill of Tara (south of Navan, Meath's county town), has more to show of its history than Louth. It is to Meath that anyone seriously interested in Ireland's past must come, to discover the extraordinary megalithic tombs of the Boyne Valley; to trace the origins of Christianity in Ireland at such places as Kells and

Monasterboice; to visit Trim Castle, the largest Anglo-Norman Castle left in Ireland; and to walk down King William's Glen to the site of the Battle of the Boyne. Here, William III's defeat of the forces of James II in 1690 meant not only the end of the Catholic Stuart cause but also changed the balance of power in Europe.

Wicklow and Kildare, along with other parts of County Dublin beyond the limits of the capital's influence, have more obvious attractions for visitors seeking to escape urban life. Wicklow, particularly, has many a fine refuge, both inland, where the peaks and valleys of the Wicklow Mountains make superb walking and mountain bike country and where there are several beautiful houses and gardens to visit, including Powerscourt and Russborough House,

both relics of Anglo-Irish life, and on the coast, where several seaside resorts of Victorian origin attract new generations of holidaymakers.

As mountains go, the Wicklows are little more than rounded, not very high hills – the highest peak, Lugnaquilla, is just over 925m (3,000 ft) and only a few granite-covered peaks, such as Great Sugar Loaf Mountain, have resisted weathering to retain a jagged shape – but what they miss out on in terms of mountain grandeur they more than make up for in the quality of their uninhabited wildness. This was once bandit country, so it is hardly surprising that the only road cutting through the Wicklows

from north to south was originally a military road, built to stop more uprisings like the 1798 Rebellion from occurring. The road still follows its original route, from Rathfarnham in Dublin's southern suburbs to Aghavannagh.

Part of the military road is also followed by the Wicklow Way, Ireland's first officially-designated long-distance walk. Also starting in Dublin's southern suburbs, the Wicklow Way follows an 132-kilometre (82-mile) course to Clonegal on the Wexford border in County Carlow, taking in some memorable locations, including Glencree, Lough Tay and Glendalough.

ABOVE
An old anchor frames a view of the lighthouse at Howth Harbour, a fishing port and yacht marina at the northern end of Dublin Bay. Before it silted up early in the 19th century, Howth was the main Dublin harbour for sailing packets from England.

OPPOSITE
Dunmoe Castle, built above the River Boyne near Navan in Co. Meath in the 16th century, was a stronghold of the D'Arcy family. Its greatest claim to fame is that Cromwell is said to have fired on it from the other side of the river in 1649.

was used for freight until as recently as 1959. The Royal Canal which also started in Dublin, but north of the Liffey, was cut through to Mullingar, reaching the Shannon by 1817. Both canals have been undergoing some renovation recently; barge and waterbus trips are run on the Grand Canal at Robertstown, north of Kildare, and there are hire cruisers available at Tullamore. Monasterevin, west of Kildare, has a particularly fine aqueduct which carries the Grand Canal over the River Barrow and attracts many canal enthusiasts.

Foremost among the rivers of the eastern counties are the Boyne, joined by the Blackwater at Navan before it flows down the lovely, fertile Boyne Valley; the Liffey, rising in the Wicklow Mountains and flowing through Kildare and into the Irish Sea at Dublin; the Barrow, which also waters part of Kildare on its southward journey to the Celtic Sea; and, in Wicklow, the Avoca, formed by the meeting of the rivers Avonmore and Avonbeg, and which reaches the sea at Arklow, a busy port and harbour town where shipbuilding has been important for several centuries: Sir Francis Chichester's *Gipsy Moth IV* was built in a yard here.

To reach Arklow, the Avoca flows down a

History Along Rivers and Canals

The eastern counties are well-off for water, with several river systems, as well as two of Ireland's fine canals within their limits.

The canals, both of which are open along sections, if not their whole lengths, to pleasure craft, are the Royal Canal and the Grand Canal. They were built in the 18th century, when Irish confidence in its country's trading future was at its height; both of them connect Dublin with the heart of Ireland on a parallel course north and south of the Liffey.

The Grand Canal, begun in 1756, was cut through Dublin south of the Liffey and had reached the Shannon by the early 19th century. It

where visitors can follow a passage, lined with standing stones, to a chamber where three recesses still hold the stone basins in which the bones of the dead, and funeral offerings of stones and beads, were kept.

Kildare also has many relics of its ancient history, especially in the basin of the River Barrow. Among them is the hilltop fort at Knockaulin, where the great circular wall surrounding the fort and a defensive ditch on the inside is an important landmark. The site, first settled in the Stone Age, was a seat of the kings of Leinster, and was inhabited, so archaeologists believe, until around A.D. 400.

Another centre of the kings of Leinster in Kildare is to be found on the wooded plain of the River Liffey. Naas, whose name translates as 'the castle of the Kings', is today the county town of Kildare, its commercial success built around the racing industry. Centuries ago, Naas, after the departure of the kings of Leinster, found itself a fortified town under Anglo-Norman rule and all that remains of the rule of the kings is a mound called the North Motte, and of the Anglo-Normans, the remains of a 13th-century castle in the grounds of the Protestant church of St. David. Perhaps more enjoyable for present-day visitors to Naas is the Canal Harbour, which was once a busy terminus with the Grand Canal and still has pleasant towpath walks.

ABOVE LEFT
An arched stone bridge crosses the River Boyne at Slane, Co. Meath.

LEFT
One of the most important passage graves in Europe, Newgrange was carefully restored between 1962 and 1975. According to Celtic lore, the kings of Tara were buried here; in fact, Newgrange is pre-Christian and predates the Kings of Tara by many centuries.

OPPOSITE ABOVE
A peaceful stretch of the Grand Canal at Mespil Road in Dublin. The canal, built in the mid-18th century as a trading link with the River Shannon, has had a new lease of life as a leisure waterway.

OPPOSITE BELOW LEFT
Winter snow dusts the peak of the 504-m (1,654-ft) Great Sugar Loaf Mountain in Co. Wicklow. A granite layer has given the mountain a distinctive peak among the Wicklow Mountains, most of which were rounded off by glacier action during the Ice Ages.

OPPOSITE BELOW RIGHT
Yellow Steeple, beside Talbot's Castle at Trim, Co. Meath, gets its name from the colour its stone turns at sunset. The steeple is all that is left of St. Mary's Abbey, once famous for the miraculous cures attributed to a wooden statue, 'Our Lady of Trim'. The statue was burnt and the abbey ruined by Cromwell's forces in 1642.

lovely valley, the Vale of Avoca, memorably described in Thomas Moore's poem, *The Meeting of the Waters*:
"There is not in this wide world a valley so sweet As that vale in whose bosom the bright waters meet."

It is a sentiment shared these days by the millions of viewers, in Britain and Ireland, of the popular television drama series, *Ballykissangel*, which is filmed in the picturesque village of Avoca, at the heart of the Vale of Avoca. Handweaving has been one of the local trades for centuries, and the weavers of Avoca Mill, founded in 1723, are believed to be putting in many extra hours' work keeping up with the demands of the stream of visitors that 'television tourism' has attracted.

Because all these rivers reach the coast at accessible estuaries, it is not surprising that they were used as a way into Ireland's heartland by Celts, Viking raiders and more peaceable Christian missionaries. Relics of their presence, from prehistoric passage graves and Viking hill forts to

medieval monasteries are to be found throughout the area.

The lovely Boyne Valley in County Meath, for instance, fertile and beautifully wooded, is just an hour's drive north of Dublin. Since time immemorial the river was a main route to the centre of Ireland from the coast, and Drogheda near its mouth an important port; consequently the area is rich in prehistoric relics of the people who once lived here and could justifiably be called the cradle of Irish civilization. Their great grave mounds, built on the north bank of the river along a stretch of the river between Tullyallen and Slane, called *Brú Na Bóinne*, 'Palace of the Boyne', and on hilltops facing towards the sun, still have the power to astonish and intrigue us today.

The prehistoric burial sites at Dowth, Knowth and Newgrange, built by the time the Ancient Egyptians began building their pyramids, are the oldest in the British Isles. Today, the most accessible to visitors is the passage grave at Newgrange, which has been carefully restored and

Christianity in the Eastern Counties

While the pre-Christian peoples of Ireland have left their mark on the landscape of the eastern counties, so, too, have those who brought Christianity to Ireland and established it as the religion of the country. Places like Kells, Monasterboice and Glendalough, whose names ring out strongly in the history of Christianity in Ireland, are all to be found in this part of Ireland, along with many relics of early Celtic Christianity, such as the high crosses at Old Kilcullen (said to be a relic of a monastery founded here by St. Patrick himself), Castledermot and Moone in County Kildare, which also has, in Kildare town, a reminder of St. Brigid. She founded a monastery here in 490, on the site of which was built the Church of Ireland's Cathedral of St. Brigid at the end of the 12th century. The massive building you see in Kildare today is a largely Victorian reconstruction, though its round tower is believed to date back to the original building.

Kells, famous for the magnificent four-volume manuscript of the Gospels, the *Book of Kells*, the illumination for which was either executed or completed there in the late eighth century, is today a busy little market town in the valley of the Blackwater river in County Meath. Its main relics of the monastery founded by St. Columba in the sixth century include a tenth-century round tower, much weathered, a stone cross and a small stone oratory called St. Columba's House. Its greatest treasure, the *Book of Kells*, has been in the Library of Trinity College, Dublin since the 17th century.

Monasterboice, also in County Meath, a few miles north of Drogheda, is the site of a monastery founded by St. Buithe (Boethius) in the early sixth century and is of particular interest among the

TOP
The ruins of Mellifont Abbey, the first Cistercian house to be founded in Ireland, in 1142, stand beside the River Mattock in Co. Louth.

ABOVE
Intricate carvings depict scenes from the Old and New Testaments of the Bible on the high crosses at Monasterboice, Co. Louth.

OPPOSITE
The 1,000-year-old round tower at Glendalough in Co. Wicklow, one of Ireland's most atmospheric monastic sites.

monastic foundations of Ireland in that it was a dual foundation, for both men and women and became a great seat of learning in later centuries. All that remains of the monastic site today are three splendid high crosses, one of them 7m (23 ft) high, and carved with scenes from the Bible.

Two other Christian sites near Monasterboice are Mellifont and the Hill of Slane. Mellifont was Ireland's first Cistercian abbey, built beside the River Mattock by monks from France in the 12th century and enough ruins remain to give a strong evocation of what the place must have been like in its heyday.

The Hill of Slane has been associated with Christianity in Ireland since its earliest days, for it was here that St. Patrick challenged druids who were holding a pagan festival at Tara one Easter Eve. He should have been put to death, but preached the gospel before the High King so eloquently that the king allowed his subjects to choose for themselves between paganism and Christianity.

One of the most atmospheric of all Ireland's many Christian sites is in Wicklow, at Glendalough, the 'valley of the two lakes'. Here, in the sixth century, St. Kevin founded a monastery devoted to learning and the care of the sick which, after his death, became a place of pilgrimage. Despite being sacked several times by the Vikings, the monastery flourished for several centuries and was still active, though very much reduced, at the time of Henry VIII's Dissolution of the Monasteries in the 16th century. Careful restoration of the site began in the 19th century and today Glendalough is an inspiring place to visit, with an excellent centre where visitors can be guided around the main places of interest and hear of the history of this very special place.

LEFT
Marley House, built as a country manor house in the 18th century, is now in the southern Dublin suburb of Rathfarnham. Its grounds are now a public park.

BELOW
Visit Malahide Castle, at Malahide on the coast north of Dublin city, and you might encounter Puck, the family ghost, said to be still living there among the treasures of this historic pile. The original castle was built in the 12th century by the Talbot family, who managed to hold on to it, apart from a few years under Cromwell, until the 1970s.

OPPOSITE
The Glen of the Downs, carved by flood waters during the Ice Ages, near Bray in Co. Wicklow, now follows the main road south from Dublin to Wexford.

Within the Pale: Houses and Gardens

It was in the counties of the Pale in the 18th century that the Anglo-Irish felt most at home and most relaxed, ready to devote time and money to creating a domestic environment in which comfort and the enjoyment of the good things of life took precedence over thoughts of invasion and warfare which had caused the Anglo-Normans to scatter the countryside with castles and towers.

Georgian-style architecture and building flourished in the eastern counties, leaving behind a splendid legacy of fine houses and gardens whose pleasures can be enjoyed by many more people today than their builders ever imagined. While many impressive buildings dating from the heyday of Anglo-Irish society have, naturally enough, fallen into disrepair or disappeared altogether, many more are still inhabited as private residences, have been turned into fine country house hotels, or are among the most popular venues for Irish tourism.

An interesting example of house turned hotel is Kilkea Castle in County Kildare, a medieval stronghold of the Fitzgeralds (much modernized and rebuilt in Victorian times, today's potential hotel guests may be relieved to know). Today's owners of another Fitzgerald house, Carton House at Maynooth, County Kildare, also have plans to turn this fine Georgian house into a hotel. It was once the country home of the 20th Earl of Kildare who, as Duke of Leinster, built the hugely grand Leinster House in Dublin, now the home of the Irish Parliament.

The Earl of Kildare's wife was Lady Emily Lennox, whose sister Louisa married into the wealthy Conolly family, owners of Castletown House, also near Maynooth, and at the top of Ireland's list of stately homes which are open to the public. Castletown and its attendant village, Celbridge, were intentionally designed and built on a grand scale to demonstrate the wealth of its owner, and much of the superbly designed and decorated interior was commissioned by Lady Louisa Conolly. Today, Castletown is in the care of the Irish Office of Public Works and is one of the most visited of Ireland's stately homes.

While County Kildare can also offer one of Ireland's most interesting gardens, the Japanese Gardens on the estate at Tully, which includes the Irish National Stud, it is in County Wicklow that Ireland's best-known house-and-garden estate, Powerscourt, is to be found. The once-splendid early 18th-century Palladian mansion was gutted by fire in 1974, but it has now been restored. It forms a backdrop to part of the magnificent gardens, although both are dominated by the dramatic peak of Great Sugar Loaf Mountain.

Not far from Powerscourt is Killruddery House, in the shadow of Little Sugar Loaf Mountain near Bray. Built in the mid-17th century, Killruddery is the seat of the earls of Meath and is today mainly visited for its superb gardens, complete with ponds, canals and a sylvan theatre, designed in formal French Classical style and laid out by a French gardener who once worked at Versailles.

It is not the gardens that take people to Russborough House, also in County Wicklow, near Blessington, so much as the magnificent collection of paintings exhibited there. The collection was the work of the 19th-century entrepreneur, Alfred Beit, a co-founder of the De Beer Diamond Mining Company in South Africa. He left the collection, including works by Rubens, Frans Hals, Velazquez, Murillo, Goya and Gainsborough, to his nephew, Sir Alfred Beit, who chose to house them in the splendidly decorated Palladian mansion, Russborough House, which he bought in 1952.

Today, it would appear that great houses are in more need of protection than they were in the 18th century, for Russborough House has been burgled twice, once by a woman in an attempt to raise funds for the IRA, and once by international art thieves. Bridget Rose Dugdale's haul was found, unharmed, on a farm in County Cork, but only a fraction of the works of art taken during the second break-in have been found, in The Netherlands.

Architecture in Ireland

A wealth of building styles are to be discovered in Ireland. Despite the actions of invading hordes throughout the centuries – Vikings, Anglo-Normans, Cromwell's army, the Black and Tans in the south, the IRA in the north, even present-day 'developers' – who have all cut destructive swathes through the island's architectural heritage, it is a wonder that so much still remains.

While much of Ireland's domestic architecture remains, as the description implies, in the form of houses that people actually live in, there is a great deal that has been carefully preserved or restored and is open to the general public. Visitors can discover for themselves, scattered the length and breadth of the country, the realities of life in Stone Age forts and Bronze Age crannogs, early Christian monasteries, Anglo-Norman castles, fine Georgian country houses and tiny, one-roomed cottages.

The entire spectrum of pre-Christian Ireland is laid before us in the remains of burial sites, including tombs, dolmens and cemeteries, and in several splendid Iron Age forts. There are also two excellent reconstructions of prehistoric buildings at Craggaunowen in County Clare and

at the Ulster History Park, a splendid open-air museum in County Tyrone.

Particularly impressive are the dolmens, or portal tombs dating from the megalithic period, including the Browne's Hill Dolmen in County Carlow, which still supports the biggest capstone in Ireland, weighing in at about 100 tonnes, and the Legananny Dolmen in the Mountains of Mourne in County Down. At Newgrange in Meath is just about the most important Stone Age passage-tomb in Europe, standing in a great area of ancient tombs known as *Brú Na Bóinne*.

The best places to see the remains of entire Stone Age settlements are at Lough Gur in Limerick and Céide Fields in County Mayo. Much of the latter site was buried and preserved under bog and archaeologists have been able to uncover enough of the remains of stone walls and farm buildings to indicate that a sizeable community once lived and farmed here.

As for Stone Age ring forts, one of the best preserved is Staigue Fort on the Iveragh peninsula in Kerry, while the Iron Age forts on the Hill of Tara, visible only as hollows and grassy mounds, remain deeply evocative of Celtic Ireland.

The earliest Christians in Ireland left few

remains because their settlements were built of perishable wattle and daub and their churches, some of them reputed to be very fine, were of wood. Later, they began to raise impressive stone crosses, magnificently carved, and many of these survive, notably at Monasterboice in County Louth, Clonmacnoise in Offaly and Kells in Meath.

The earliest stone churches, most of them with thatched roofs, were single chambered with a west door and small east window; a particularly fine example of a rare stone-roofed single-chamber church is the Gallarus Oratory on the Dingle peninsula in County Kerry.

With marauding Vikings on the rampage throughout the land, people living in and around Christian monasteries began to build slender, tapering round towers of stone. Some were intended as bell towers, but many were seen as places of refuge and for storing precious manuscripts. Often, the entrances were high up above ground level, accessible by ladders which could be hauled back up into the tower if need be.

About 70 round towers still survive in Ireland today, many of them in a surprisingly good state of repair. The perfectly preserved, 25-metre (82-foot) tower on Devenish Island in County Fermanagh, the even taller tower by the ruins of the Romanesque-style St. Declan's Cathedral at Ardmore in Waterford and the Temple Finghin tower at Clonmacnoise monastery in Offaly are three examples. The round tower at Timahoe in County Laois, rising 30m (100 ft) above the village (and a wood notable for its noisy colony of rooks) is famous for the elaborate carvings around its entrance arch, which is set 5m (16 ft) above the ground.

There is also a round tower among the many monastic buildings at Glendalough in Wicklow, a particularly atmospheric Christian settlement begun by St. Kevin in the sixth century which functioned as a monastic settlement right up to Henry VIII's Dissolution of the Monasteries in the 16th century.

The round towers of the Celtic Christians were built between the 10th and 12th centuries; by the end of this period, the Anglo-Normans were moving into Ireland in increasing numbers, their castles beginning to appear throughout the countryside. The earliest castles in Ireland were of the Norman motte and bailey type, involving a wooden tower on a raised mound surrounded by a ditch, so familiar to the Anglo-Saxons in England. Later, the Anglo-Normans began to erect much more formidable square stone keeps which grew into mighty castles, such as Trim and Carrickfergus.

Then, in 1429, Henry VI offered a £10 subsidy for anyone constructing a castle of a given minimum size in Ireland. Thus began the period of the tower house, more fortified residence than castle, examples of which were built all over Ireland between the 15th and 17th centuries. Among the most visited of these castles today are Bunratty Castle in Clare and Blarney

Castle in County Cork. Thoor Ballylee, near Gort in County Galway, is famous as W. B. Yeats' summer home for most of the 1920s.

The 18th century was a period of relative stability and quiet for Ireland, during which the ruling Anglo-Irish no longer felt the need for fortified houses. They began to build country mansions in Palladian or Neo-Classical style, some of which were constructed around existing castles: but many of them were designed from scratch by such architects as Richard Castle (originally Cassels) and James Wyatt. Most of them were surrounded by walled gardens and parks, where a gracious, comfortable life-style could be maintained in surroundings of often considerable luxury.

Today, the style and grandeur of these great houses can be best appreciated by visits to Mount Stewart in County Down, Malahide Castle in County Dublin, Rowallane in County Down (headquarters of the National Trust in Northern Ireland), Bantry House (overlooking Bantry Bay in County Cork), and splendid properties like Powerscourt, Castletown House and Russborough House – all built within reach of Dublin at a time when it was the centre of the Anglo-Irish world.

OPPOSITE
The Hook Head lighthouse, at the southern tip of the Hook Head Peninsula, the eastern side of Waterford Harbour, marks the site of the oldest lighthouse in Europe and one of the oldest in the world. The first warning light was a beacon, lit here by monks in the fifth century.

TOP
The Great Sugar Loaf dominates the skyline in this view of part of the 20 hectares (50 acres) of formal gardens at Powerscourt, one of the great estates of Ireland, in Co. Wicklow.

ABOVE
One of the finest possessions of the National Trust in Northern Ireland, Mount Stewart, near Newtownards in Co. Down, is a fine 18th-century mansion surrounded by a superb garden.

Chapter Three
The South and Southeast –
Wexford, Waterford, Carlow, Kilkenny and Tipperary

Not for nothing was the original Gaelic name for Ireland's southeast corner *Cuan-na-groith*, 'haven of the sun'. This region of fine river valleys, fertile agricultural land – perhaps at its finest in the Golden Vale in Tipperary – and scenic hill country, with a coast lapped by the warm waters of the Gulf Stream, boasts the highest hours-of-sunshine count in Ireland.

It also has some of the loveliest beaches in the country, several of them fringing popular holiday resorts on the east coast, and there is good walking country for the more energetic all over the region, including the Galtee Mountains in Tipperary, the Knockmealdowns in Waterford, the South Leinster Way in Carlow, Kilkenny and Tipperary, the Munster Way between Carrick-on-Suir and Clonmel, and the southern section of the Wicklow Way in County Carlow. Little wonder, then, that the region still experiences great invasions every year, though now, instead of Vikings and Anglo-Normans, the invaders are holidaymakers, both Irish and from abroad, with Rosslare Harbour, a major port for ferries from Wales and France, the first sight of Ireland for a great many of them.

Centuries ago, the majority of Viking and Anglo-Norman invaders of Ireland, as at least one Christian missionary before them, also had their first glimpse of the country from the St. George's Channel and the Celtic Sea. They chose to come this way because the natural harbours and river estuaries of the southeastern coast offered, via several fine river valleys, direct routes into the heartland of Ireland.

The Vikings found a land with few towns (the Celts were herders of cattle and growers of crops rather than town dwellers) but with a well-established network of Christian monasteries, for St. Declan is reputed to have first set foot in Ireland at Ardmore in County Waterford a generation before St. Patrick returned from France in 432. At that time, control of the countryside was in the hands of the Celtic kings and although the Vikings destroyed many monastic and other religious foundations, many more survived, outstanding among them being the monastery and chapel built on the great limestone outcrop, the Rock of Cashel on the Tipperary plain, which was also the seat of the kings of Munster and is today one of the important relics of the early Christian period in Ireland.

Three of the five present-day counties in the region, Wexford, Carlow and Kilkenny, were at one time part of the ancient province of Leinster. Waterford, while also part of Leinster at one time, was for most of the period of the kings of Ireland part of Munster, along with Tipperary.

It was a 13th-century king of Leinster, Dermot MacMurrough, who 'invited' the Anglo-

Normans into Ireland. Richard FitzGilbert de Clare, Earl of Pembroke, widely known as Strongbow, entered Ireland in 1170 by way of Waterford harbour, into which flow three of the great rivers of the southeast, the Nore, the Barrow and the Suir. Further east, the Slaney, flowing into Wexford harbour, begins its journey to the sea far to the north in the Wicklow Mountains – another way into the heartland for any raider arriving on Ireland's southern shores.

Strongbow beseiged Waterford, a Viking town of some size and importance, for three days before overcoming it. He then consolidated his position by marrying King Dermot's daughter, Aoife. Their marriage was celebrated in Reginald's Tower, built in Waterford by the Viking chief Ragnvald (or Reginald) the Dane at the beginning of the 11th century. The tower, having survived an attempt by Cromwell to capture it, has in its time been a mint, a prison and an army barracks; today, a showpiece of Waterford's tourist industry, it is the town's Civic Museum.

OPPOSITE
Reginald's Tower, part of Waterford's city walls, which were originally built by the Vikings and greatly extended by King John in the 12th century, has recently been restored to give today's visitors a glimpse into its medieval origins.

BELOW
Evening sunlight gives a golden glow to the roofs and steeples of the city of Wexford and to the waters of the Slaney.

The Vikings in the Southeast

Scattered across the region, much of it fertile agricultural country today, are a few reminders of its Viking past and a great many of its Anglo-Norman heritage. Although the ridge of granite of the Wicklows and Blackstair Mountains tended to set up a natural barrier in prehistoric times between the people living on the fertile plain between mountain and sea and those living beyond the mountains in Carlow and Kilkenny, the existence of several rivers, carving fine valleys through the mountains and across the plains, meant that the Vikings, arriving in their longboats

from Norway and Denmark early in the eighth century, were able to penetrate far inland from the island's southeastern coast.

The two main coastal towns here, Wexford and Waterford, like Arklow and Wicklow further north, were both important Viking trading posts. Wexford's Viking name, *Waesfjord*, means 'the harbour of the mudflats' and Waterford's *Vadrefjord* means, appropriately enough, 'weather haven'. Both Wexford and Waterford still show, in the pattern of their narrow streets, strong signs of the Vikings' centuries of occupation. Waterford, now more famous for its fine crystal than its past

history, is still able to show visitors, as well as Reginald's Tower, several fragments of the fortified wall the Vikings built after their arrival in the ninth century.

While Wexford town has very few relics of its ancient past remaining, and owes its regular 'invasion' as much to visitors to its famous international Wexford Opera Festival as to its history, the county has managed to recreate its past at the excellent Irish National Heritage Park, built at Ferrycraig, a few miles up the Slaney from Wexford harbour. Here, visitors can experience daily life in ancient Ireland, including a

reconstruction of a Viking settlement, complete with thatched round houses made of mud, straw and animal skins, set behind wood and straw palisades. A Viking longboat is moored nearby on the Slaney, the longest of the rivers flowing into the sea at Wexford.

Viking raiders left their mark much further inland, too. A grim reminder of the effects of a Viking raid recently came to light in the Dunmore Cave, situated in the limestone country north of Kilkenny, which has a good share of Irish myth and legend attached to its many caverns and stalactite-hung galleries. The bones of 50 people,

mostly women and children and dating from the early tenth century, were found in the cave in 1973. The fact that none of the skeletons had broken bones suggests that the people were taking refuge from a Viking raid, only to die of starvation or, perhaps, suffocation (if the Vikings had tried to smoke them out).

ABOVE
The Irish National Heritage Park at Ferrycarrig, beside the River Slaney in Co. Wexford. The conical-roofed buildings surrounded by a palisade in the foreground are parts of reconstructed crannogs, first built in the Bronze Age as defensive homesteads.

OPPOSITE
The harvest is complete on this farm below the Blackstairs Mountains near the village of Borris in Co. Carlow.

Anglo-Normans Leave Their Mark

If the Vikings left few obvious signs of their presence in this part of Ireland, the Anglo-Normans left a great many, often buildings on land given them by the Crown, partly as a means of controlling the country. Great castle builders, the Anglo-Normans were also strong supporters of the church – though they never hesitated to destroy any monastery whose occupants failed to toe the Anglo-Norman line – and in many places castle and monastery, with its attendant place of worship, existed virtually side by side.

From Cahir (also spelt Caher) in County Tipperary to Enniscorthy in Wexford, from Dungarven and Lismore in County Waterford to Kilkenny, ancient castles, some in ruins, some restored and some with more modern buildings on their medieval foundations, still have plenty to tell us about the Anglo-Normans and their successors. One or two do not, however: Carlow, well-sited on the River Barrow and therefore of strategic importance, was once dominated by a massive early 13th-century pile. All that is left of it today, hidden in the grounds of a mineral water factory, are a couple of towers and a bit of wall. Far from being one of the many 'ruins that Cromwell knocked about a bit', to quote Marie Lloyd's song, Carlow's castle survived to the 19th century in

good enough condition for a local doctor to consider turning it into a mental hospital. Unfortunately, in a praiseworthy attempt to get as much fresh air into his castle hospital as possible, he chose to use gunpowder to enlarge the windows in the thick walls and succeeded in reducing most of the castle to a pile of rubble.

Though there is little left of Carlow Castle, there are many others with much to attract visitors. Cahir Castle and Ormond Castle at Carrick-on-Suir, both in County Tipperary, could be film sets, they look so fine, Cahir with its square keep and crenellated walls on a rock in the middle of the Suir, and Ormond Castle, in contrast, all gabled and mullioned, as befits a building often called 'the finest Elizabethan manor house in Ireland'.

Down in County Waterford, Lismore Castle, originally built, like Dungarvan Castle at the handsome port of Dungarvan, for Henry II's son John (the King John of Magna Carta fame) offers yet another view of Irish castles. Set proudly on a cliff above the Blackwater, Lismore is not all it appears to be. In the 19th century its owner, the sixth Duke of Devonshire, brought in his old friend, Joseph Paxton, builder of the Crystal Palace (as well as additions to the duke's ancestral pile, Chatsworth in Derbyshire) to rebuild Lismore Castle. Today, the castle, still owned by the

Devonshires, is of interest because of its superb garden, where the Elizabethan poet, Edmund Spenser, is thought to have composed part of *The Faerie Queene*.

Spenser also had connections with Enniscorthy Castle in Wexford, which was briefly leased to him by Queen Elizabeth, so flattered was she by his great poem. Enniscorthy Castle today houses the County Wexford Historical and Folk Museum but, for many people, the castle houses something much more intangible than mere museum relics. The final, and bloodiest, struggle of the 1798 Rebellion was fought almost at the castle's feet, on Vinegar Hill, where the rebels held out for a month. The castle preserves many relics of the battle, and perhaps something of its atmosphere, too: local people say that if you climb Vinegar Hill of a summer's evening and stand by the windmill where the rebels made their last stand, the sounds of the battle will be wafted to you.

Although Enniscorthy has had a castle since the 12th century and has had Christian connections for much longer, St. Senan having founded a monastic settlement here in the sixth century, it cannot show today the sort of living connection between medieval church and Norman castle which makes Kilkenny, for instance, so interesting.

Around Kilkenny

Kilkenny, the county town and in the mid-17th century virtually the capital of Ireland, is the most outstanding medieval town in Ireland, its centre dominated by St. Canice's Cathedral, named after the saint who founded a monastery here in the sixth century, and Kilkenny Castle, built by Strongbow's son-in-law, William, Earl of Pembroke, between 1192 and 1207 on a site dominating the River Nore and the surrounding countryside. Between the two mighty buildings lies a centuries-old street pattern cut by narrow alleys of obviously medieval origin. Among them are many historic gems, ranging from Black Abbey, the medieval church of a Franciscan friary, to a 14th-century inn, Kyteler's Inn, and the Elizabethan Rothe House, now Kilkenny's local museum.

While Kilkenny carefully preserves its medieval past, to the delight of thousands of visitors every year, it also fosters a fine artistic tradition. The Kilkenny Arts Festival, held every August, is now one of the most important in Ireland.

Most visitors to Kilkenny also find time to visit the monastic sites in the Nore valley. The ruins of Kells Priory, founded by Augustinian friars from Bodmin in Cornwall and later rebuilt behind a strongly fortified enclosure, are

extensive, as are the ruins of the Cistercian Jerpoint Abbey, near Thomastown, another once-fortified medieval settlement. Jerpoint Abbey still has among its ruins the effigies of two bishops and, in its fine cloisters, many remarkable carvings, the detail of which gives fascinating glimpses into the medieval past of this part of Ireland.

ABOVE
The old mill on the River Nore at Bennettsbridge in Co. Kilkenny houses one of Ireland's many excellent potteries, the Nicholas Mosse Pottery, which produces earthenware with attractive spongeware patterns.

RIGHT
Impressively set above the River Nore, the Norman fortress of Kilkenny Castle, seen here from its rear lawns and courtyard, dominates the city of Kilkenny as it has done since the 12th century.

The Irish and their Horses

horses has been part of the fabric of life in Ireland for centuries and kings, both legendary and historic, had their private racing greens. Horse fairs and public assemblies gave ordinary folk the chance to take part in racing, too. Although a ban by Oliver Cromwell on Sunday racing, followed by the upheavals in Irish life after the Battle of the Boyne put a distinct dampener on racing, steeplechasing began quietly to fill the gap and by the mid-18th century was well-established in Ireland, with hundreds of race meetings taking place all over the country. The first race to be officially called a steeplechase took place in 1752, when two men raced each other between Buttevant and Doneraile in County Cork, using the spire of St. Leger Church in Doneraile as a guide to their finishing post.

Today, there is virtually year-round racing at some 280 meetings in Ireland, whether racing on the flat, National Hunt racing, or point-to-point, and of course, there are always Irish horses grabbing attention in racing outside Ireland, particularly in England, where an Irish horse first won the Grand National in 1880 and the Derby some 20 years later. Needless to say, Ireland has its own Grand National and Derby, both first run in the 19th century.

Among the highlights of the Irish racing calendar are the National Festival of Steeplechasing at Punchestown, 20 miles from Dublin, in April; the Irish Grand National, run on Easter Monday at Fairyhouse in County Meath; the Irish Derby at the Curragh, County Kildare, in

The internal combustion engine may have long since seen off the horse as a main means of transport in Ireland, as everywhere else, but in Ireland particularly, the horse remains an essential preoccupation of Irish life and society. The reasons are partly historical and partly a natural phenomenon.

Stone Age farmers are thought to have been the first to introduce the horse to Ireland, about 4,000 years ago. Much later, Celtic invaders brought horse-drawn chariots with them. At the end of the 16th century, Spanish Arab horses, washed ashore from the ships of the Armada wrecked on Ireland's western coasts, are thought to have interbred with the native Connemara pony, producing a horse of surpassing hardiness and speed.

The sturdy Connemara pony, along with the Irish Draught, which gives Irish showjumpers, eventers and hunters their strength and great jumping ability, are among nature's reasons for the pre-eminence of the horse in Irish life. Others are the mild climate and the country's underlying limestone, which gives the soil calcium and minerals, essential for building strong bones. Then, of course, there is that indefinable extra, the affinity between man and horse which seems stronger in Ireland than anywhere else.

Early in the 1990s an official count showed that there were about 55,000 horses in Ireland, of which nearly a quarter were racehorses. Racing

June/July; and the uniquely Irish Laytown races, run on the beach at Laytown, south of the Boyne estuary, in July or August, depending on the state of the tide. Then there are a whole string of important race meetings during the year at Leopardstown, a racecourse in Dublin's southern suburbs, and at three summer festivals of racing in County Kerry, at Killarney, Tralee and Listowel.

The thoroughbred industry in Ireland is centred on the Curragh, a grassy plain in County Kildare, where many of the country's studs and training yards are situated. The Irish National Stud was established at Tully on the western edge of the Curragh in 1945 with its main aim the improvement of the quality of bloodstock in Ireland. The stud had been formed in 1900 by an eccentric Anglo-Irish breeder, Lord Wavertree, who, believing in the powers of astrology, had skylights installed in the stables to ensure that the power of the moon and stars would get to his horses.

Today, parts of the Stud are open to visitors, and there is a museum where can be seen, among other things, the skeleton of the great Irish steeplechaser, Arkle, who won England's Cheltenham Gold Cup three times in a row in the 1960s; and it must not be forgotten that Red Rum, another three-times winner of a great English steeplechase, the Grand National, was also Irish-bred.

For all enthusiasts of equestrianism, whatever their favoured discipline, the social highlight of the year is the Dublin Horse Show in August, which attracts contestants, particularly to showjumping, and spectators from all over the world. Many of the horses competing here will have been purchased at Ireland's bloodstock sales, the most important of which are at Kill, County Kildare or at the main national hunt sales, the Tattersalls Sales, at Fairyhouse in County Meath.

To the average horse-lover, however, the best and most enjoyable horse sales are the traditional non-thoroughbred fairs which have been part of Irish life for centuries. The oldest and most famous of these in Ireland, and once one of the three greatest horse fairs in Europe, is Galway's Great October Fair, held at Ballinasloe. Back in the 18th century, agents of the great powers of Europe came to Ballinasloe to buy cavalry horses – including, so tradition has it, Napoleon's horse Marengo (though this is denied by those who run the July horse fair at Cahirmee in County Cork, which also claims to have supplied Napoleon with his famous steed). Today, the Great October Fair is a lively occasion offering thousands of visitors horse racing and street entertainment as well as the horse sales.

ABOVE
The Horse Fair of Spancilhill, near Ennis in Co. Clare, has been held in June every year since its charter was first granted in the 17th century.

OPPOSITE ABOVE
They're off! Another race starts at one of Ireland's 25 race tracks.

OPPOSITE BELOW
Improving the quality of Irish bloodstock is the main aim of the Irish National Stud at Tully in Co. Kildare.

Chapter Four
The Midlands –
Monaghan, Cavan, Longford, Westmeath, Offaly and Laois

The Hill of Uisneach, between Mullingar and Athlone in County Westmeath, is considered, at least by local people, to be at the geographical centre of Ireland (people living further south near Birr in County Offaly also make the same claim). The famous Catstone on the Hill of Uisneach once marked the point of intersection between the five great provinces (or kingdoms) of ancient Ireland, Connacht, Munster, Leinster, Meath and Ulster. Present-day Monaghan and Cavan, along with Donegal further west, are the only counties of the old province of Ulster not to have been included in the new province at Partition.

Stand on the flat top of this not particularly high hill – 190m (620 ft) at its highest point – and you can certainly see much of these ancient provinces: on a clear day, it is said, you can see as far as the O'Connell Monument in Dublin's Glasnevin Cemetery, more than 145km (90 miles) away. Much of the view from the hill is of quiet, green tranquillity, full of farming communities.

The country of these six Midland counties is characterized by grassland and peatland, or raised bog country (as distinct from the blanket bog of the west of Ireland), especially in County Offaly, set between Boora Bog in the west and the Bog of Allen in the east. It is dotted with many loughs, while part of the border land between Laois and Offaly is fine hill country, popular with walkers and hikers, the main range of which are the Slieve Bloom Mountains. Legend says that these were formed when the music of a west Laois piper caused the trees and rocks to jig vigorously up and down.

Although the mountains are not very high – the highest point, Alderin, reaches only 526m (1735 ft) – the country is rugged and desolate enough to give a real feeling of wilderness. Try walking the 30-kilometre (20-mile) circular Slieve Bloom Way, one of a couple of dozen well sign-posted walks in the mountains, and you will encounter woods, moorland and bog, trace a section of one of the old high roads to Tara and follow the bed of a pre-Ice Age river valley. If you are lucky, you may also see such wildlife as the Irish hare, the rare pine marten, fallow deer and even mountain goats, as well as many species of birdlife.

Hill country of a different kind – the small, rounded hills known as drumlins, shaped by the ice and glaciers of the last great Ice Age – is a characteristic of Cavan and Monaghan. Many of these drumlins show signs of prehistoric habitation, for the tops of hills were good places to built fortified settlements, and the remains of countless ancient tombs and ring forts are dotted over them, most of which have been left undisturbed for centuries.

The two most prominent architectural features of Athlone, county town of Westmeath, are the 19th-century Church of Saints Peter and Paul and the 13th-century Norman castle, set near each other on the west bank of the Shannon.

A Country of Rivers and Loughs

Many of the people who built these settlements
were able to penetrate the interior of Ireland by
means of its rivers and streams, for this is a region
of many waterways, loughs and canals.

The two great canals of the region are the
Royal Canal, cutting west across Westmeath and
Longford from Dublin to reach the Shannon
upriver of Lough Ree, and the Grand Canal, also
coming out of Dublin, but further south through
Offaly. The Royal Canal has been undergoing
major restoration work in recent years, and has
some pleasant towpath walks along its banks,

from places like Ballymahon and around
Mullingar, Westmeath's county town, which the
Royal Canal almost encircles. The Grand Canal is
well supplied with companies hiring out pleasure
cruisers and narrowboats from many of the towns
and villages along its course. One of them,
Tullamore, the county town of Offaly, actually
owed much of its 19th-century prosperity to the
Grand Canal, which reached the town in 1798.

In County Cavan, a third great canal system
has taken shape in recent years. This is the
realization of an old dream, to link the Shannon
and Erne rivers with a canal and thus create a

major waterway system in the Midlands. The
scheme is centred on Ballyconnell in north-west
Cavan, where the Woodford river is a link in the
scheme, and Ballinamore in County Leitrim. The
Shannon-Erne Waterway has been open since
1993, providing a system of rivers and linking
canals to transport waterborne holidaymakers
through Cavan.

Cavan, in which the two great rivers, the
Shannon and the Erne, both have their sources, is
said to have as many loughs as there are days in
the year. Much of the heart of Westmeath is dotted
with loughs, including Sheelin (shared with

County Cavan), Lene, Derravaragh, Owel and Ennell. Many of these are familiar names in Irish folklore. Lough Derravaragh, for instance, is said to have been the home for 300 years of the children of the King of Lir, turned into swans by their jealous stepmother. Today, it is not folklore so much as the fine fishing in the lough, as well as the splendours of nearby Tullynally Castle, home to ten generations of the Pakenham family, earls of Longford, which bring visitors here.

County Longford, bordered in the west by the Shannon, also has numerous loughs which, though they may be of little interest to the average tourist, attract many anglers and watersports enthusiasts, as do rivers like the Inny, well-known for its coarse fishing and its trout.

One of the largest loughs of the Midlands is Lough Ree, where the borders of Longford,

Westmeath and Offaly meet. The River Inny, flowing into Lough Ree southwest of Ballymahon, a town with many associations with Oliver Goldsmith, is just one of many attractive waterways in the region. Also notable in and on the shores of Lough Ree is Inchcleraun, an island whose six churches are the remains of a large monastery founded in the sixth century by St. Diarmuid, and Saint's Island (now a peninsula) on which are the ruins of a 14th-century Augustinian monastery. At lovely and peaceful Barley Harbour, tucked away at the end of a pensinsula on the lough's eastern shore, is a haven popular with people cruising the lough and the Shannon, and also the workshop of a sculptor, Michael Casey, whose fine carvings in ancient, semi-petrified bog wood have earned him an international reputation.

OPPOSITE
Pleasure boats moored on the Shannon at Clondra in Co. Longford.

BELOW
On the Shannon-Erne Waterway near Ballinamore. The waterway, which links Upper Lough Erne in Co. Fermanagh and the River Shannon at Leitrim, follows the channel of a canal which fell into disuse in the mid-19th century and which was repaired and reopened in 1993.

Historical Highlights

Many names on the map of the Midlands of Ireland have strong historical associations. One with links to early Irish history, and with a place in Irish folklore as well, is the Rock of Dunamase, rising out of the Laois countryside east of Port Laoise, the county town.

The Rock is an ancient site, included on Ptolemy's famous map of A.D. 140, and has seen many battles for possession of the fortress on its summit. The Vikings plundered it, the Anglo-Normans built a castle on it, and the O'Moores, who had been clan chieftains in the area before the time of St. Patrick, built another one, called Masg Castle (or Dun Masg) in the 15th century. This one was destroyed by Cromwell's army in the 17th century – despite the presence, legend has it – of a huge mastiff called Bandog, whose flame-throwing jaws were said to be the animal's main weapon for protecting the treasure reputed to be buried under the rock. Perhaps Bandog's presence had some effect, however, for the castle was not

completely destroyed, and its remains are still as attractive to walkers today.

A name closely associated with early Christian history in Ireland is that of Clonmacnoise in west Offaly. Here, one of the largest monasteries to be built in Ireland was founded by St. Ciaran, coming down the Shannon from his first monastery on Hare Island in Lough Ree, in the mid-sixth century. Carefully sited on a fertile meadow by the Shannon, with the only way to it, apart from the river, a ridgeway walk called the Pilgrim's Road, the monastery survived and flourished as a centre of learning for 600 years.

Some of Ireland's finest illuminated manuscripts were produced at Clonmacnoise, including the 11th-century *The Book of the Dun Cow* (*Lebor na hUidre*), the earliest-known manuscript to have been written in Irish, which took its name from a cow belonging to St. Ciaran. Another treasure from Clonmacnoise is the magnificent Crozier of Clonmacnoise, with a gold handle inlaid with silver and decorated with

animals. It can now be seen in the National Museum in Dublin.

The ruins at Clonmacnoise are extensive and well-preserved and include a cathedral, eight churches, a castle, two round towers and three high crosses. A collection of some 200 grave slabs, many inscribed with memorial prayers in Irish, can be seen in the Visitor Centre, together with the three high crosses, replicas having replaced them in their original locations.

One of the eight churches at Clonmacnoise was built by a chieftain's wife called Dervorgilla. It was her abduction by Dermot MacMurrough, King of Leinster, which led first to the king's overthrow then to his cry for help to the Anglo-Normans, only too ready to oblige him: Dervorgilla built her church in 1167, and the

Anglo-Norman Strongbow was in Waterford with his army in 1169.

Two other Christian places in the region must also be mentioned. At one of them, Durrow Abbey, north of Tullamore in Offaly, little remains of a place called a 'noble monastery' by the Venerable Bede. The abbey's greatest contribution to Irish culture, the *Book of Durrow*, a superbly illuminated manuscript dating from the seventh century, is now in the Library of Trinity College, Dublin.

There is more to see at Fore, in the exceptionally lovely Fore Valley in County Westmeath. At Fore itself is an ancient church believed to date back to the time when St. Fechin built a monastery here around A.D. 630. Local legend has it that the saint himself placed the huge

lintel, carved with a rare Greek cross, over the church's west door, using the power of prayer to get it there. This feat is one of the 'Seven Wonders of Fore', which among others include such things as water that flows uphill, water that will not boil, wood that will not burn and a monastery built on quaking sod. The last one is easily explained, for the Benedictine priory at Fore was built on reclaimed bogland. As for the rest, local people are happy to explain them, and there are even discussions about making a regular tourist trail round them.

ABOVE
Cloghan Castle, just outside the pleasant little town of Banagher, Co. Offaly, where the young Anthony Trollope worked as a surveyor for the Post Office, has been inhabited without interruption for 800 years.

OPPOSITE ABOVE
The Cross of the Scriptures and the 19-m (62-ft) Round Tower are just two of many relics of early medieval monastic life to be seen at Clonmacnoise, established on a remote stretch of the Shannon by St. Ciaran in the mid-sixth century.

Music in Ireland

There is a very strong tradition of music-making in Ireland – to sing as well as to dance to, music to set the feet tapping. It is not the kind of music designed to be performed before an audience who are expected to applaud politely once the piece is finished. Irish music means participation and this is what happens – in pubs and bars, set-dances, sessions (*seisiún*) and festivals (*fleadh*) – the length and breadth of the island.

Traditional Irish music, grown out of the music-making and story-telling traditions of the bards of pre-Christian, Celtic Ireland, has survived some fierce knocks over the centuries, not least the turbulent times of Cromwell and William III, when the bard's role in Irish music was all but wiped out, and the Potato Famine of the 19th century drove a large part of the rural-dwelling, music-making community abroad to the United States and the English-speaking colonies of the British Empire.

Today, traditional music thrives in Ireland, helped partly in the Republic by the government's sponsoring of Irish-language radio and partly by a continuing dedication to ballad-singing in all those Irish communities abroad, in the United States and in many countries of the old British Empire, from Australasia to southern Africa.

The establishment of Comhaltas Ceoltóirí Eireann (CCE) in the Republic in 1951, aimed at the promotion of traditional music, has also played a large part in helping the music survive. There are now several hundred branches of the CCE organizing regular informal sessions to which everyone is welcome. Larger than the sessions are the festivals, held all over Ireland. The greatest of these is the All-Ireland Fleadh, held at the end of August in a different town every year.

You'll find notices for sessions and festivals, as well as pub sessions, in local newspapers and in tourist board listings. Keep an eye open as you walk past bars, too – most of them put notices in their windows announcing their forthcoming events. Depending on where you are in Ireland, the music on offer could be ballads, laments and airs; jigs, reels and hornpipes, taken from a national repertoire, according to a 1985 count, of more than 6,000; and *sean-nós*, a form of unaccompanied singing in Gaelic.

The best traditional Irish music sessions to join are the smaller ones, where, if you are lucky and everyone is in the right mood, there will be a splendid mingling of music and 'crack' (good fun and conversation). Unless you are at one organized by the tourist board, you are unlikely to hear the Irish harp being played, despite the fact that this ancient instrument is a national symbol. Instead, the music will be played on the *uilleann* pipes (a more sophisticated version of Scotland's bagpipes), a fiddle and a tin whistle, with a hand-held drum called a *bodhrán* providing the beat and rhythm. Some groups may also include guitar, accordian, flute and piano.

Since the 1960s, this traditional Irish music scene has been taken to a much wider audience by musicians inspired by the traditional music group Ceoltóirí Cualann; and later The Chieftains. With them came The Clancy Brothers in Aran sweaters, taking America by storm, and The Dubliners.

The tradition for making music is so strong in Ireland that it is not surprising that the country has made a big contribution to other types of music as well. There were so many Irish winners of the Eurovision Song Contest in the 1980s and 1990s that it began to look as though Dublin would soon be a permanent home of the event.

At the same time, Irish rock music was making its mark on the world's music scene, with singers like Van Morrison and Sinéad O'Connor

OPPOSITE
The fiddle and the bodhrán, a frame drum usually made with goatskin, are important instruments in traditional Irish music.

ABOVE
U2, who have been hailed as the world's greatest rock band; they recorded their breakthrough album, The Unforgettable Fire, *in Ireland, mostly at Slane Castle in Co. Meath.*

ABOVE
Singer Sinéad O'Connor, holding yet another award.

and groups such as U2, the iconoclastic, punk London-Irish The Pogues, and The Cranberries becoming hugely popular. The last-named group's lead singer, Dolores O'Riordan, retains, like Van Morrison and Sinead O'Connor at their best, strong echoes of the traditional Irish *sean nos* in her singing.

It is an echo that some Irish rock musicians may perhaps deny, maintaining that they are rebelling against traditional Irish music, 'rammed down their throats from childhood'.

In fact, Irish music today, in whatever form, traditional, rock, pop or soul (the music celebrated in Alan Parker's splendid film *The Commitments*), though firmly based in the past, is as enjoyable as ever and is a great part of the pleasure of visiting Ireland.

Musicians at a music festival in Ennis, principal town of Co. Clare, a county renowned for its music. Ennis hosts several festivals, or fleadhs, *every year.*

Chapter Five
The Southwest –
Cork and Kerry

At Ireland's southwest corner the coastlines of Cork and Kerry reach out into the Atlantic in a series of jagged-edged peninsulas, all with islands at their tips and separated by long, wind- and sea-swept bays, inlets and river estuaries. Ranges of hills and mountains form barriers down the peninsulas, including the Caha Mountains on the Beara Peninsula, shared by Cork and Kerry; Macgillycuddy's Reeks, with Ireland's highest peaks, on the Iveragh Peninsula; and the Slieve Mish Mountains which dominate the eastern end of the Dingle Peninsula. Further inland, the Boggeragh Mountains, scattered with ring forts, standing stone circles and other prehistoric remains, separate the southern part of Cork, Ireland's largest county, from its northwestern corner, a remote, thinly populated area watered by the upper reaches of the Blackwater river.

Despite the region's relatively easy access, by sea at least, to and from Europe – a fact recognized by invading Vikings and Anglo-Normans a thousand years and more ago, by Christian missionaries before that, and by such supporters of Irish rebellion as the Spanish and the French much later – this part of Ireland was for many centuries a remote area, far removed from the influences of sophisticated society and intrusive government.

One result of this was the survival of the Irish language in the far west long after it had either been suppressed or simply fallen out of use in favour of English elsewhere in the country. Today the region is known as a *Gaeltacht* – or Irish-speaking – with the language surviving particularly strongly in the Dingle and Iveragh peninsulas in Kerry and near Macroom in County Cork. Irish culture, especially music and literature, thrives in the region today: there are even Irish language summer schools with some students from Europe.

Tralee's famous Rose of Tralee International Festival and the annual Puck Fair at Killorglin, on the Ring of Kerry, show two, quite different, present-day aspects of the southwest's Gaelic inheritance. Yet another aspect of this is the traditional music scene, alive and well in hundreds of pubs and clubs. Cork, especially, is renowned for its music, with traditional music very much to the fore in pubs and bars – though it takes something of a back seat at the end of October every year, when Cork's famous international jazz festival gets into its stride.

Leaving Remoteness Behind

The one part of the southwest which, in terms of location, could be seen as the most remote part of Ireland but which is in fact, because of its extreme beauty, a magnet for visitors, is Killarney. At the heart of County Kerry, this glorious land of island-studded lakes, wooded valleys, rolling hills and

OPPOSITE TOP
Lough Leane, largest of Killarny's lakes, with Macgillycuddy's Reeks beyond, seen from the air.

OPPOSITE BELOW
Rain can't dampen the spirits or the atmosphere at Cork's annual jazz festival, held every October.

LEFT
Muckross House and gardens, set in the splendidly car-free Muckross Estate, is one of the highlights of a visit to Co. Kerry's Killarney National Park.

BELOW
Sea-angling, yachting, and excellent food in a cosmopolitan atmosphere are among the attractions of Kinsale, on Co. Cork's fine coast.

BOTTOM
The world's oldest yacht club, the Royal Cork Yacht Club, may have moved across Cork Harbour to Crosshaven, but Cobh (pronounced 'Cove') remains a delightful yachting town, as well as home to a sizable fishing fleet.

lush forest, 10,000 hectares (25,000 acres) of it in the Killarney National Park, has been the greatest tourist attraction in Ireland since the mid-18th century. First promoted as such by a local magnate, Lord Kenmare, in 1750, when the Romantic movement was just beginning to take a hold in Europe, Killarney proved to be the right place at the right time.

Although Killarney still holds the number one spot on Ireland's tourism chart, other parts of the southwest, notably the spectacular coastline, have been greatly increasing in popularity in recent years, both with the Irish themselves and with visitors from Europe, more than eager to visit a country which combines beauty with an unhurried way of life where the influence of the Gulf Stream allows fragile wild flowers and the Mediterranean strawberry tree (or arbutus) to flourish.

The southwest's long coastline, all the way round from Youghal, an ancient fortified harbour and now a popular seaside resort on the Blackwater estuary, to Tarbert on the Limerick border, where the Shannon river reaches the sea, is heavily indented, creating hundreds of extra miles of bays, inlets, estuaries and harbours. While this coast has a rich maritime history and a strong tradition of fishing, still to be seen operating out of harbours from Dingle in County Kerry to Ballycotton in Cork, it is also a paradise for bird-watchers, for yachtsmen and for the many who just like to walk on remote, unpopulated sandy beaches where the only sounds are of the sea and of seabirds stalking the foreshore or wheeling in the sky above.

Maritime history and the pleasures of yachting come together in many small ports all along Cork's coast, notably at places like Youghal, Cobh and Kinsale. Cobh, Cork city's port, was once an important stopping-off place on the transatlantic shipping run and was for thousands of Irish emigrants to North America and Australia their last sight of their homeland. The *Sirius*, making the first steamer crossing of the Atlantic, began her epic trip from Cobh, and the ill-fated *Titanic* called here in 1912. In contrast, Cobh can also boast of once possessing the world's oldest yacht club, the Royal Cork, founded in 1720.

Kinsale is a characterful town with a colourful history, which includes the Battle of Kinsale in 1601, in which O'Donnell and O'Neill chieftains, aided by a Spanish force, made a last stand against English rule, only to be defeated. Kinsale is another sailing haven on the south coast to have experienced a tourist boom in recent years and its annual regatta is an important event in the social calendar of southern Ireland. Further west along the coast, places like Baltimore, sheltered behind Sherkin Island and with a boatbuilding yard and sailing school, and Skibbereen are harbours which attract yachts and small pleasure craft. Out to sea, beyond Sherkin Island and Clear Island, is a point of special interest to serious yachtsmen, the Fastnet Rock. This is the western turning point for one of the world's great yacht races, the Fastnet Race, which is held every two years and starts from Cowes on the Isle of Wight.

Around and About Cork

Cork is Ireland's second-largest city, a harbour city and the cultural capital of the south. Most of the city's business and shopping centre is built on an island, well inland of the River Lee's estuary, with many of the streets built over former boat channels. The first famous settler here was St. Finbarr, who founded a monastery on the Lee in the seventh century. On the site of his monastery today is Cork's fine 19th-century Church of Ireland cathedral, its three Gothic spires rising above surrounding buildings near the Lee's south channel.

Although Cork, unlike Dublin, has few places of importance to visitors, it is a most attractive city to walk about. There are plenty of fine Georgian buildings, attractive quays and bridges to stroll along, busy markets, one or two interesting art galleries and plenty of pubs and bars. The Triskel Arts Centre is one of the main venues for Cork's important international film festival, held in early October every year. It is followed at the end of the month by the renowned Cork International Jazz Festival, so Cork in October is a lively place.

Beyond Cork city's limits, County Cork stretches away in a semi-circle of gentle landscape and fertile farmland with rivers winding down heavily wooded valleys offering fishermen much fine angling. Dotted across the landscape are some ancient castles, including 15th-century Blarney Castle, where the famous Blarney Stone, set in the castle's battlements nearly 30m (90 ft) above the ground, offers the gift of eloquence to anyone able to kiss it.

There are also some fine examples of the Anglo-Irish legacy in this part of the country. Near Cobh is the Fota Wildlife Park and Arboretum, in which many kinds of exotic animals, including apes, cheetah, giraffe and zebra, have the run of the 18th-century landscaped park which surrounds the classically elegant Fota House.

North of Cork and beyond the valley of the Blackwater river, in a quiet area known as the Golden Vale, are several more castles and houses of interest, including the fine Doneraile Court, once home of the St. Leger family and another mansion whose fine park is home to a wildlife reserve, and Kilcolman Castle, once lived in by Edmund Spenser and his family, but a ruin since it was burnt down by a mob in 1598: Spenser and his wife escaped the fire, but their infant son did not.

The horse is still king in this part of County Cork, with Buttevant, a market town four miles west of Doneraile, hosting the large Cahirmee Horse Fair every July. Both Buttevant and Doneraile have important places in the history of Irish horse racing, for the first recognized steeplechase took place here in 1752, starting at Buttevant Church and finishing at St. Leger Church in Doneraile, the latter church's steeple providing a marker for the riders. Mallow, on the Blackwater, has one of the four important race courses in the southwest, the other three being at Listowel, Tralee and Killarney.

Much further west, where Cork assumes the increasingly wild and far more elemental landscape typical of Ireland's southwest, Bantry House, overlooking the superb natural harbour of Bantry Bay, is another fine example of Irish Georgian architecture, still inhabited by the descendants of the earls of Bantry, who built it. From Bantry House's superb gardens, visitors can look across Bantry Bay to the Beara Peninsula where, beyond the Caha Mountains, lies County Kerry.

OPPOSITE
Cork's impressive Protestant cathedral, St. Finbarr's, was built in the mid-19th century to a design in the French Gothic style by William Burges. It is the third cathedral on the site, though there have been chapels and churches here since the sixth century.

BELOW
These houses on Cork's Grand Parade, one of the city's main commercial thoroughfares, date from the 18th century.

The Kenmare River and the Ring of Kerry

The Kenmare river is an inlet of the sea, cutting a deep cleft into the coast of Kerry between the Beara and Iveragh peninsulas. Other, smaller rivers and streams drain into it, notably the Finnihy, the Roughty and the Sheen near its head, and the Sneem which reaches the Kenmare near the pretty village of Sneem. On either side of the Kenmare rise mountains, among which, on the southern side, lies the beautiful and tranquil Inchiquin Lough amid splendid scenery. There is a flourishing plant life here, including, on the lough's southern shore, an area of primeval sessile oaks, called Uragh Wood. There is even a spectacular waterfall, falling from another lake in the hills above Inchiquin Lough. Because of the Gulf Stream, sub-tropical plants grow everywhere, palm trees, yuccas, bamboos and fuchsias showing in profusion alongside rhododendrons, the strawberry tree (arbutus), yellow gorse and green oaks and willows.

It is all so very charming that it is not surprising that villages like Sneem seem to have sprouted as many tourist cafés and gift shops as brightly-painted houses, while the resorts of Parknasilla, on the southern section of the Ring of Kerry, and Kenmare, a busy and attractive market town, seem far more cosmopolitan than one would have suspected. Although Kenmare is a fine example of 17th-century town planning, having been founded in 1670 by Cromwell's Surveyor-General in Ireland, Sir William Petty, it is in a place where many antiquities, including a 3,000-year-old stone circle, attest to long habitation. The lacemaking industry for which Kenmare, guided by the nuns of the local convent of Poor Clares, became famous in Victorian times is undergoing something of a revival today.

One reason why Kenmare has so many visitors in summer is because it is on the Ring of Kerry, one of the world's great scenic routes, which circles the Iveragh Peninsula, with its spectacular mountain and coastal scenery and its crowning glory, the Killarney National Park. The Ring of Kerry is just about everything one could expect of a world-famous region of supreme natural beauty.

There are other fine resorts, like Waterville, a favourite holiday haunt for Charlie Chaplin and his family, Valencia Island, reached by a modern bridge from Portmagee and able to claim that it is the most westerly harbour in Europe, and Derrynane, whose wide, sandy beaches stretch for miles. There is the amazingly well preserved Staigue Fort near Caherdaniel, one of the best in Ireland. And there is the island group, the Skelligs, within a pleasure boat's cruising distance off the tip of the peninsula. Great Skellig offers the hardy tourist, via a 150-metre (500-foot) climb up a stone stairway built a thousand years ago, a view of a particularly magnificent monastic site, complete with some remarkably well-preserved stone beehive huts, in which the monks lived. Little Skellig is a sea-bird sanctuary, home to hundreds of thousands of gannets, kittiwakes, petrels, and their like.

LEFT
A lovely point on the Ring of Kerry: Upper Lake and Macgillycuddy's Reeks, near Killarney.

BELOW
Seabirds skim and soar over the sea and the spiked tops of the Skellig Islands, off Co. Kerry's southwest tip. Little Skellig Island, on the left, is a bird sanctuary, with the world's second largest gannet colony, and landing is not permitted. Great Skellig Island, also called Skellig Michael can, however, be visited. A stiff climb up stone steps, first hacked out by St. Finian and his monks 1,400 years ago, brings the visitor to the remains of the monastic site Finian founded.

The Dingle Peninsula

While the Dingle Peninsula cannot offer the same dramatic impact as the Iveragh Peninsula, it has for many an attraction all its own, not least the wonderful peace of its splendid landscape, which includes the Connor Pass, Ireland's highest mountain pass. This seems specially so at the height of summer, when the jaunting cars block the roads out of Killarney and the way to every lake, every tourist site, every view becomes a slow-moving trek: much more agreeable to think about hiring a horse-drawn caravan in Tralee and take off at a gentle pace to discover the Dingle Peninsula.

It is easy to feel you have gone back in time. This is partly due to the remoteness and peace of the place and partly because the peninsula west of Dingle town is a *Gaeltacht*, where Gaelic is the first language of most of the inhabitants. There are also something like 2,000 prehistoric and early Christian sites to be found here, giving an overpowering sense of history and of the past. Among the finest of these is the extraordinarily atmospheric Gallarus Oratory, a remarkable little dry-stone building, shaped like an upturned boat, its interior lit by one small window and a narrow door. Set in a field a short distance inland from Smerwick Harbour, the oratory is thought to have been built between 800 and 1200.

The solitariness of the Gallarus Oratory seems a world away from the busy, colourful life of Dingle, the fishing port and tourist centre on the south side of the peninsula. Dingle, which for walkers wishing to take their time getting there, is 32 km (20 miles) from Tralee via the Dingle Way, has had an eventful history, including a period when it was a centre for smuggling. Among its tourist attractions today is a dolphin called Fungie who has been delighting spectators with his antics since the early 1980s.

Tralee, at the head of Tralee Bay on the northern edge of the Dingle Peninsula, is County Kerry's chief town. It is in the lovely, fertile Vale of Tralee, celebrated in the song 'The Rose of Tralee', which gives its name to the Rose of Tralee International Festival. Fenit, west of Tralee on the north shore of Tralee Bay, was the birthplace of St. Brendan the Navigator. Legend has it that Brendan began his epic voyage in a curragh to cross the Atlantic to North America from the south coast of the Dingle Peninsula. In 1976-77, the British writer/adventurer Tim Severin proved that the saint could have done it by building a replica curragh of wood and leather 11m (36 ft) long, which he named the *Brendan*, and sailing it across the Atlantic, retracing Brendan's route.

OPPOSITE
The Blasket Islands can be seen outlined on the horizon from Clougher Strand on the Dingle Peninsula in Co. Kerry.

BELOW LEFT
Paudie's Bar is typical of the many bars, restaurants and B&Bs which welcome tourists to Dingle, main holiday town of Dingle Bay.

BELOW
The Gallarus Oratory has survived the elements in this remote part of the Dingle Peninsula for 1,200 years. Built as a place for quiet, private prayer, the Oratory remains a movingly evocative Christian site.

Wild Ireland

Ireland packs into its relatively small size a wonderful variety of scenery and many areas of unspoiled grandeur. There are some 2,000 miles of coast, with hundreds of islands scattered off-shore, including some very wild coast indeed, in the southwest, where the land reaches out into the Atlantic Ocean in a series of finger-like peninsulas whose cliffs and rock stacks provide havens for many colonies of birds.

Away from the coast is a country of glorious contrast: mountains in the west, with much of the land between covered by blanket bog, one of the finest examples of which lies in the Slieve Bloom Mountains in Laois and Offaly; green and purple hills and valleys; and, at the island's centre, a fertile lowland region of wetlands and lakes watered by many lovely rivers and streams. Very little is left of the great broadleaf forests which once covered much of the land, and the long-distance views are likely to be filled with lush, rolling pastureland, the result of plentiful rainfall, divided into a checkerboard of hedge-lined fields where livestock graze.

Much of Ireland's farming, especially in the west, is still along traditional lines, which is of great value in helping wildlife to survive in good numbers. Ireland was cut off from the rest of the British Isles and Europe by rising sea levels after the last Ice Age, and many animals, common in Europe, are unknown in Ireland as a result.

You won't encounter any snakes when walking in Irish grassland, for instance, nor will you see moles, weasels or the common toad or any small rodents other than the wood mouse. You should see more red squirrels than grey ones, for the former are more widespread, while in hill country, especially in Connemara, you should see red deer, an introduced species. On remote beaches on western islands grey seals breed and sometimes that nocturnal animal, the otter, may be seen during the day, so undisturbed are these places. Although the otter's preferred habitat are the shallow seas off rocky coasts, it is also known on Ireland's inland waterways.

For many nature lovers, however, the great interest of Ireland lies in its birdlife. Both on the coasts and along inland waterways, this is abundant. From the cliffs of the extreme west, where the chough still breeds well while declining in the rest of Europe, to the mudflats and salt marshes of east- and south-coast river estuaries which attract spectacular flocks of wading birds and wildfowl, including Brent geese, curlews, redshanks and teal, Ireland is a bird-watcher's paradise.

If observing colonies of breeding seabirds, including kittiwakes, shags, Manx shearwaters, gannets and several different types of gull is what interests you, then you should be positioning yourself on some west-facing headland in early summer. You might even be rewarded with dolphins or porpoises coming within sight of land.

Ireland's rivers and central wetlands, created by the high annual rainfall, offer breeding grounds for many kinds of water birds, including swans, herons and moorhens. Along the Shannon

and the Erne rivers are many areas of bird-attracting wetland, and the larger lakes in the north offer breeding grounds for birds like the elegant great crested grebe.

There are five national parks in the Republic of Ireland. Unlike Britain's, Ireland's national parks are all state-owned and are not very big. What they lack in size, however, they more than make up for in the varied nature of their landscapes and geology and the richness of their fauna and flora. The five parks are the Glenveagh National Park, set in the spectacular mountain ranges of County Donegal; the small but carefully conserved Connemara National Park in County Galway; the beautiful, lake-dominated Killarney National Park in Kerry; the Wicklow National Park; and the strangely austere and even bleak Burren National Park in County Clare, where the limestone grassland gives shelter to an

extraordinary collection of wild flowers, from arctic-alpine species to Mediterranean ferns. Although far from finished, the Burren Way already offers walkers a dramatic path through The Burren and along the tops of one of Ireland's most spectacular sights, the Cliffs of Moher.

Northern Ireland, while it has no national parks, does have several officially designated areas of outstanding natural beauty, and can offer walkers a superb introduction to its scenic beauties by way of the Ulster Walk, a complete circuit of the six counties nearly 900km (560 miles) long. And Northern Ireland's scenic beauties are well worth discovering, from the lovely Mourne mountains in southeast County Down to the spectacular piles of basalt which make up the Giant's Causeway on the northern coast of County Antrim.

ABOVE
Ireland's coastline, with its long stretches of rugged cliffs broken by river estuaries and sand-dunes, provides homes for a wide range of seabirds. Puffins nest in large colonies on many rocky cliff sites.

RIGHT
A gannet guards its young on the Saltee Islands, off Kilmore Quay in Co. Wexford. The Saltees are one of Ireland's most significant bird sanctuaries, with important colonies of gannets, cormorants, guillemots, kittiwakes, auks and puffins. The time to visit is late spring and early summer: by July-August, however, most of the birds have flown and the islands are very quiet.

OPPOSITE
In the rugged Comeragh Mountains, in the north of Co. Waterford. Much of this country is the same red sandstone which lies under the most scenic parts of Cork and Kerry.

Chapter Six
The West –
Limerick, Clare, Galway, Mayo and Roscommon

BELOW: From Croagh Patrick, Co. Mayo, Ireland's holiest mountain and colloquially known as the Reek, there is a splendid view across island-studded Clew Bay.

RIGHT: On the Cliffs of Moher, which rise to almost 230m (700 ft) at their highest point on the coast of Co.Clare.

Ireland's western counties, though they have much in common, not least in their long stretches of dramatic coastline and, as far as history goes, a certain remoteness from the affairs of government in the east, also have their own distinctly different atmospheres.

The counties in the south, Limerick and Clare, share the lower reaches of the River Shannon and its largest lake, Lough Dergh, as their outstanding geographical features. The area bordering the Shannon, Ireland's longest river, and much of it of great beauty, has known human habitation for at least 7,000 years: a canoe, recently found in the Shannon Estuary mudflats, has been carbon-dated to 4800 B.C., which sets it in the Mesolithic period. From about the fifth century A.D., this area was part of the province of Munster, though the seat of the Kings of Munster was further away, on the Rock of Cashel in present-day Tipperary. More recently, it has become increasingly popular with visitors and holidaymakers, attracted to its numerous riverside resorts.

Away from the Shannon, Limerick and Clare seem quiet counties, and provide a breathing-space for tourists hurrying from the scenic glories of Kerry to those of Galway. But Limerick has in its county town of Limerick, founded by Norsemen, the only urban area of city size in the region – in fact, Limerick is the fourth largest city in Ireland. County Clare is famous for the liveliness of its music scene and both counties can offer many attractions along their spectacular,

jagged coastline, not least the Cliffs of Moher and the Burren in Clare, and the Aran Islands, scattered across the mouth of Galway Bay.

What most people imagine to be the typical west-of-Ireland landscape is in fact to be found further north, in Galway, Mayo and Roscommon, once the heart of the historic province of Connaught. Bordered by a rugged coastline is a sparsely populated land of dour, bracken-covered hills, peat bogs, and fields divided by stone walls, which typifies the landscape of Connemara in the west of Galway. Inland, where Galway and Mayo merge into Roscommon, is extensive and fertile agricultural and cattle-rearing country, dotted with quiet lakes.

But these western counties are changing, too. These days, the medieval streets of Galway town resound to the voices of students at the thriving Galway university college and of workers in the new high-tech industries which have been developed there. And at nearby Knock, just over a 100 years ago a quiet little village in the middle of a bog in County Mayo, they have had to build an airport, with a jumbo jet-size runway to cope with the million and a half tourists they get every year. Most of them come to worship at the shrine of Knock where two local women are reputed to have seen visions of the Virgin Mary, St. Joseph and St. John the Evangelist in 1879, but there are also increasing numbers of people flying in to Connaught Airport in order to visit Ireland's west country.

Around the Lower Shannon

For other modern travellers, the first sight of
Ireland may well be the broad sweep of the
estuary of the Shannon, seen from the air as their
aircraft, flying in from over the Atlantic, makes its
approach to Shannon International, the world's
first duty-free airport. It is historic aviation
country here, in fact, for Foynes, on the south
coast of the estuary, was in the 1930s the
European airbase for the transatlantic flying boat
service to Newfoundland.

This area has a history much longer than that
of modern aviation, of course. There are several
important Stone Age sites in the region, notably
round Lough Gur, south of Limerick, which is one
of northwest Europe's most complete Stone Age
and Bronze Age sites, with a gallery grave dating
from 2000 B.C., stone circles, forts and the
foundations of many huts still to be seen. The
barren limestone country of the Burren, further
north in County Clare, also had many megalithic
remains, of which the best-known, the
Poulnabrone Dolmen, has been dated to 2500 B.C.

His engagement in excavations around Lough
Gur inspired the archaeologist John Hunt to create
his own prehistoric site in County Clare, the
intention being to provide the people of the 20th
century with an insight into how their Celtic
ancestors lived in the Bronze Age. Today, the
Craggaunowen Project, created in the grounds of
Craggaunowen Castle, at Kilmurry, is a very fine
example of how past history can be vividly
recreated for our benefit. Visitors can see people
in the costume of the period engaged in activities
such as spinning, potting and cooking, and they
can walk round a typical crannog – a man-made
island, built as a defensive dwelling, usually in a
lake and enclosing wattle-and-daub houses which
was still being built in Ireland until the end of the
16th century. Also at Craggaunowen is Tim
Severin's *Brendan*, in which he re-enacted the
sixth-century voyage of St. Brendan the Navigator
to North America.

Signs of early Christian settlement are also to
be found here, among them a sixth-century

stone, which is inscribed in Ogham (the earliest Irish script) and with Nordic runes.

Cratloe House, west of Limerick, is a rare example of an Irish long house, in which all the rooms are interconnecting. The whole of the Bunratty Folk Park, on the road from Limerick to Shannon Airport, has many important buildings, including the formidable Bunratty Castle, recently magnificently restored and offering medieval banquets to tourists, and a complete 19th-century village street. The pretty town of Adare, south of Limerick, has many interesting buildings, including a 12th-century Augustinian abbey (now Church of Ireland), a Trinitarian priory (used by Catholic worshippers) and numerous 19th-century thatched cottages.

Limerick itself was a Viking settlement, established in the ninth century on an island between the Shannon and the smaller Abbey river, which the Anglo-Normans turned into a thriving town. They embellished it with some splendid buildings, including a superb cathedral, St. Mary's, and King John's Castle, both prominent buildings in the town today, despite the castle's turbulent history, having been subjected to capture by the unruly O'Briens, kings of Thomond, in the 13th century, bombardments by Cromwell's General Ireton and by William of Orange's troops later on in the 17th century.

County Clare's county town is Ennis. Much smaller than Limerick, it remains an attractive

town with many brightly-painted houses and shops, its winding lanes recalling its medieval origins, of which the ruined but still impressive Ennis Friary is the main survivor today. Ennis was another town of the O'Briens, kings of Thomond, and their rebellious spirit lived on well after their passing, so that even in the 19th century Ennis remained a proud bastion of Irish nationalism. The town's main street and main square are named after Daniel O'Connell, The Liberator, who was elected M.P. for Clare in 1828. A monument to him dominates O'Connell Square.

ABOVE
Magnificently restored Bunratty Castle, the fourth or fifth fortified building on this site on the River Ratty in Co. Clare, has turned its early 15th-century origins to good use in the 20th century, offering visitors medieval banquets and the pleasures of a Folk Park in the extensive grounds.

LEFT
The Poulnabrone Dolmen, a megalithic tomb, was erected on the craggy limestone of the Burren in Co. Clare some 4,000 years ago.

monastery founded by St. Senan on Scattery Island, off the southern coast of Clare near Kilrush, the county's second-largest town and an important trading centre. Later religious orders, notably the Cistercians, founded numerous monasteries in the region. Coming to more modern times, there are many historic buildings in the area, covering a wide range of architectural styles and periods.

Killaloe, County Clare, in a lovely setting where the Shannon flows out of Lough Dergh, is today a fine pleasure resort and boating centre, but it also has a lot of history behind it, not least in its impressive St. Flannan's Cathedral, which includes among its treasures an unusual Ogham

airstrips and there are ferry services from Rossaveel and Galway in County Galway and Doolin in Clare: but the old way of life, so superbly recorded by Flaherty, is fast disappearing into a world of heritage centres – there is one in Kilronan – and the business of keeping tourists occupied and happy. But while tourism, complete with jaunting cars, minibus tours and bikes for hire, is today an important money-earner for the Aran islands, older occupations, including fishing, farming and the production of the distinctive Aran knitwear continue to flourish.

LEFT
Life is quiet on Inishmaan, one of the Aran Islands to have inspired the work of Irish playwrights.

BELOW
Teetering on the edge: the concentric rings of the Stone Age fort of Dun Aengus were built on cliffs rising 92m (300 ft) out of the Atlantic on Inishmore, largest of the Aran Islands.

Galway Bay: The Aran Islands

There are three Aran islands, Inishmore, at 13km (8 miles) from end to end the largest, Inishmaan and Inisheer; *inish* is the Irish word for 'island'. The islands, stretched across the mouth of Galway Bay, are the peaks of a ridge extending from the limestone country of The Burren in County Clare.

Despite – or perhaps because of – their isolated position, the islands have long been inhabited. There are stone forts scattered across all three islands; Dun Aengus, a great Iron Age fort on Inishmore's south coast, with three concentric stone walls and a ring of spiked stone stakes as its defences, is recognized today as one of the great prehistoric sites of Europe. Christian missionaries were here early, too, St. Enda arriving in the fifth century to begin a long tradition of austere monasticism. The saint, after a lifetime of teaching, is said to have been buried on the site of his monastery where the ruins of the later St. Eany's Church are still to be found, south of Kilronan, the island's main town and port.

Like the Blasket Islands, off the Dingle Peninsula, where the Gaelic literary tradition has influenced modern Irish writing, the Aran Islands, with their continuing observance of traditional Irish culture and use of the Gaelic language, have also had a notable influence on modern Irish writing, especially drama. J. M. Synge was inspired by Aran Islands stories to write *Riders to the Sea*, set on Inishmaan, and *The Playboy of the Western World*. A present-day writer who is influenced by the life of the islands is the playwright Martin McDonagh. His recent play, *The Cripple of Inishmaan*, is based on the arrival on Inishmore in 1934 of the great documentary film maker, Robert Flaherty, come to film *Man of Aran*.

Today, as everywhere else, the Aran Islands are no longer remote – all three islands have

Around Galway

The city of Galway is the gateway to Ireland's most extensive region of *Gaeltacht*, and includes the Aran Islands, Connemara and Joyce Country. It is a lively university city with a flourishing arts scene and a busy port. It is also undergoing something of a modern high-tech industrial revolution. All of this makes Galway's county town and the biggest conurbation in the west of Ireland a place well worth visiting. It has an attractive city centre, built along the banks of the River Corrib, its own 'Latin Quarter', and a quieter area called The Quays, where Spanish traders once unloaded their ships' cargoes. There is a fine medieval church, the Collegiate Church of St. Nicholas, where Columbus heard Mass before setting out across the Atlantic in search of the New World, as St. Brendan the Navigator had done before him.

Galway, along with Clifden on the Connemara coast and Westport in County Mayo, are popular with visitors and tourists as bases from which to explore the glories of the region.

In the attractive countryside to the east and south of Galway, there are many historically interesting places to visit, ranging from the delightful fishing village of Kinvarra, on Galway Bay, to the inland market town of Portumna. South of Galway is Gort, famous for its associations with W. B. Yeats. His friend, Lady Gregory, with whom he founded the Abbey Theatre in Dublin, lived at nearby Coole Park; also on the Gregory estate is Thoor Ballylee, a tower house which belonged to Yeats and where he and his family spent their summers for many years.

Anglers and seekers of peace and tranquillity tend to head north out of Galway to island-dotted Lough Corrib, one of the chain of loughs which divides the wilder, western side of Galway and Mayo from the fertile eastern farmlands. Walkers and ramblers, along with watersports enthusiasts, tend to head for the islands, including, away to the north off Mayo's coast, Achill Island, which is Ireland's largest island and connected to the mainland by a road bridge, and Clare Island in Clew Bay, once the stronghold of a pirate queen called Grace O'Malley. But for most visitors, the region not to be missed is Connemara.

Bogland, lakes and mountains, dominated by the peaks of the Twelve Bens, watered by tumbling streams and fringed by a wild and rugged coastline, are all unforgettable features of the Connemara landscape. Some of the most spectacular scenery, including four of the Twelve Bens, lies within the boundary of the 2,000-hectare (5,000-acre) Connemara National Park. Here, Connemara ponies roam, along with red deer, re-introduced into the area, and a wide variety of birds. There are sign-posted walks and the services of botanists are available to describe the flora of the region to visitors, which includes Mediterranean, alpine and subarctic species.

Part of the National Park was once within the estate of Kylemore Abbey, a wildly romantic Gothic castle built by a wealthy Manchester businessman in the 19th century on the shores of Kylemore Lough, on the northeastern edge of the National Park. The fantasy castle became an abbey during the First World War, when a group of Benedictine nuns from Belgium took refuge there. The nuns are still there today, running a convent school.

ABOVE
Kylemore Abbey, on the shores of Kylemore Lough in Co. Galway, was built in the Gothic style in the 19th century. It is now a girls' school.

BELOW
This doorway, a superb example of Hiberno-Romanesque decoration, adorns Clonfert Cathedral in Co. Galway. It was carved with human and animal heads in the mid-12th century.

Celtic Inheritance: Irish Folklore

Wherever you go in Ireland, it is almost impossible not to encounter the island's enormously rich and pervasive folk heritage. Climb a hill, study some geographical feature or even a natural object like a tree, or stand beside a lake or in front of a ruined castle, church or monastery, and there will be someone around to tell you of the things that may – or may not – have happened here in the often far distant past.

You might be told, for instance, that the Giant's Causeway in County Antrim was made by the mighty hero Finn MacCool to provide himself with stepping stones to Scotland; or that Tory Island, off the Donegal Coast, was once the home of Balor of the Evil Eye, leader of a race of sea pirates called the Fomhoire; or that the tragic children of the King of Lir spent 300 of the 900 years they were condemned to exist as swans on Inishglora, off the coast of Mayo and yet another 300 on Lough Derravaragh in County Westmeath.

All these stories were first given currency many centuries ago and grew out of the fact that the Celts (or Gaels), coming to Ireland from Europe in the early Stone Age (around the third century B.C.), brought with them a strong story-telling tradition, but no written language. Their history was passed down the generations by word of mouth and their priests, the druids, spent many years of their training committing the stories to

memory so that they would be preserved forever. Alongside the history and story-telling aspect of Celtic culture ran a strong supernatural vein, growing out of the Celts' belief in many gods and their belief that certain aspects of their natural surroundings – trees, rivers and springs – were sacred. Thus, their lore was full of superstition, which expressed itself in stories of fairies, leprechauns and banshees.

Christianity, reaching Ireland in the fifth century, had a rapid effect on Irish folklore, for there soon began a great interplay between the oral traditions of the Celts and the written traditions of the Christian monks. The vernacular literature of Ireland, the oldest in Europe, can be dated from about the sixth century, when the tales of pre-Christian Celtic folklore, many of them no doubt altered to fit the Christian ethic under which the people now lived, began to be written down. Because the Celts were a warrior race, their tales were full of the doings of heroes and warriors.

Cúchulainn (the Hound of Ulster) was the most famous warrior in Irish folklore, beginning his heroic life by killing the savage hound of Culainn the Smith when he was only seven. Cúchulainn is supposed to have used a hurling stick as his weapon, thus indicating the ancient Gaelic origins of the popular sport of hurling. Then there was Finn MacCool (or Fionn Mac

Cumhaill) a great warrior of the time of King Cormac Mac Airt, said to have reigned at Tara in the third century. Finn, from his fortress on the Hill of Allen in County Kildare, led his band of hunter-warriors, the Fianna troop, and his great hound Bran, into many heroic exploits.

Scholars have grouped the ancient Irish sagas into four cycles. The first, the Mythological Cycle, comprises stories about the people who lived in Ireland before the Celts, and includes the story of the Battle of Moytura and the famous tale of the Children of Lir. The Children of Lir is a 'wicked stepmother' story, the stepmother being the second wife of the King of Lir, who was so jealous of the king's children that she turned them into swans, condemning them to live as such for 900 years. So potent is this story that, even today, it is illegal to kill a swan in Ireland.

Cúchulainn was the leading character in what is now called the Ulster Cycle, which recounted the deeds of the Red Branch Knights. Navan Fort, near Armagh, is believed to be the remains of the fort and settlement called Emain Macha, capital of ancient Ulster, which features in the Cycle, and one of its best-known stories, 'The Cattle Raid of Cooley', was one of the earliest tales of Irish folklore to be written down.

The exploits of Finn MacCool and the Fianna are the basis of the Ossianic Cycle, sometimes called the Fenian Cycle. Ossian (or Oisin) was Finn's son and a poet as well as a warrior. Ossian chose to enter *Tír n Óg*, the 'Land of Eternal Youth', to be with the beautiful Niamh of the Golden Hair. After 300 years there, he yearned to return home, which he eventually did after numerous exploits. Back in Ireland he met St. Patrick and recounted to the saint all the stories he knew about his father, the Fianna, and *Tír n Óg*: hence the Ossian Cycle.

The fourth group of sagas, the Historical Cycle, or the Cycle of Kings, tells stories of the kings of Ireland, and is probably part history and part fiction.

The deeds and actions of the early saints in Ireland have also contributed to the country's rich store of folklore. Many tales are told of the miraculous doings of the saints, which are easy to dismiss as myth or legend until someone comes along to demonstrate that they might well be true, as did Tim Severin when he successfully retraced the sea route St. Brendan is said to have taken across the Atlantic to North America.

The fact that Irish folklore lives on in Ireland today is largely due to the revival of interest in the island's Gaelic past in the 19th century. The Gaelic League, a non-sectarian and non-political organization was set up in 1893 with the declared aim of reviving the Gaelic language and returning to Ireland's cultural roots. Government support after the establishment of the Irish Free State ensured that the speaking of Gaelic was seen as a matter of national pride, and remains so today. However, a knowledge of Gaelic is not essential for anyone wishing to read the stories of old Ireland, for new versions of the tales are published regularly in English.

ABOVE
Navan Fort (Emain Macha) in Co. Armagh, was built by Queen Macha and, it is believed, became the capital of ancient Ulster and the seat of the kings of Ulster for 600 years.

LEFT
The 'Giants's Organ' on the Giant's Causeway in Co. Antrim, long associated with stories of the hero Finn MacCool.

OPPOSITE
The Hill of Tara, rising gently out of the plains of Co. Meath, has held a special place in Irish history and folklore for nearly 5,000 years.

Chapter Seven
The Northwest –
Donegal, Sligo and Leitrim

For many centuries, there was little to link the three counties of Ireland's northwest corner. Geographically, Donegal's wild inland mountain country and its dramatic coastline of towering, precipitous cliffs skirted by golden beaches with wind-torn spits of land jutting out into the Atlantic, has been regarded as very different from the quieter, rural charms of Sligo and Leitrim. Historically, there was a great difference, too, in that Donegal was a county of the province of Ulster, whereas Sligo, a county with an ancient tradition of Celtic history and myth, and Leitrim were within the province of Connaught.

Partition in 1921 wrought a change, however, when all three counties became part of the Republic. Despite its historical closeness to the other counties of Ulster and the fact that the county had always looked to Derry (Londonderry) as its main city, Catholic-dominated Donegal seemed an uneasy bedfellow for the new Northern Ireland with its Protestant majority.

In today's Ireland, Donegal is still something of a county apart. Those golden beaches still look as if they have never known holiday crowds, despite the numerous small seaside resorts which dot the coast. Inland, much of the centre of the county is dominated by mountains bisected by long, narrow glens. To the north, the untamed beauty of the Derryveagh Mountains, dominated by the quartzite cone-shaped peak of Errigal Mountain, adds to Donegal's apparent remoteness from 20th-century life. To the south, the Blue Stack Mountains can be explored along many miles of scenic routes and mountain walks through glens and valleys, by lovely loughs and glorious mountains.

RIGHT
Evening light falls on Co. Donegal's 752-m (2,466-ft) Errigal Mountain and the village of Dunlewy at its foot.

PAGE 66 TOP
A corner of the flower-filled gardens which surround Glenveagh Castle, Co. Donegal.

BELOW
Grianán of Aileach, a stone fort on top of Greenan Mountain in Co. Donegal, was already 1,700 years old when Ptolemy showed it on his map of Ireland in the second century.

PAGE 67 TOP
Dunree Castle stands sentinel over Lough Swilly, north of Buncrana.

BELOW
A colourful row of houses in the village of Rathmelton, on the Fanad Peninsula.

born painter and art collector, Derek Hill, and his collection of 20th-century works includes paintings by the Tory Island Primitives and by Renoir, Degas, Picasso, Kokoschka, Braque and several Irish artists, including Jack B. Yeats.

Further down Gartan Lough's southern shore is the Colmcille Heritage Centre, Church Hill, a reminder that St. Columba (*Colmcille* in Irish) was born near here in 521. In the modern building is a finely detailed exhibition on the life of the saint and an impressive collection of stained glass. Just off the road from Glenveagh to Gartan Lough is a large cross marking the saint's birthplace and an ancient stone slab, known locally as the Flagstone of Loneliness, upon which Columba is reputed to have slept. In doing so, he imbued the stone with the miraculous power of lightening the burden of sorrows of anyone lying upon it. Archeologists rather disappointingly declared the stone to be part of a Bronze Age gallery tomb but this did little to deter people, however, during the harrowing period of mass emigration, from coming here the night before their departure in the hope of alleviating their despair at leaving home.

The largest town of Donegal's central region, and a good point from which to tour, is bustling Letterkenny. Although the county town is Lifford, to the southeast, it is Letterkenny, set on the River Swilly just above the spot where the river flows into Lough Swilly, that features in the guidebooks

Among Donegal's Central Glens

The remoteness of inland Donegal is, in fact, more apparent than real. The finest scenery of the Derryveagh Mountains lies at the heart of that very 20th-century, environment-conscious phenomenon – a national park. This one is the Glenveagh National Park, which covers nearly 10,000 hectares (25,000 acres) and includes the beautiful valley of the River Glenveagh, flowing into Lough Beagh, and the marshy valley called Poisoned Glen (because Balor of the Evil Eye, the Celtic god of darkness, was slain here by Lugh, the god's single eye poisoning the ground on which it fell). There is a visitor centre in the park, from which minibuses transport visitors not wishing to walk through the park's glorious landscape to Glenveagh Castle, on the shore of Lough Beagh.

Glenveagh Castle, built of imposing granite in 1870 by John George Adair, infamous for his eviction of the tenants of several small-holdings here during the Great Famine, now belongs to the Irish National Parks Service, having been returned to the people, as it were, by its last owner, the American art dealer Henry McIlhenny, in the 1970s. The castle is well worth a visit, not only for its splendid interior, but also for its formal gardens.

Another house in the area with plenty to interest is Glebe House, 6km (4 miles) south of the National Park visitor centre by road – or three miles by way of a walk over the mountain bog tops, for Glebe House overlooks Gartan Lough, in the next valley east from Glenveagh Park. Glebe, a Regency house is also set in beautiful gardens, but these are generally of less interest to visitors than the fine paintings housed in the purpose-built gallery. Glebe House was home to the English-

as Donegal's main commercial centre. The town's long main street is dominated by the 19th-century, Gothic-style St. Eunan's Cathedral with its imposing steeple. There is also an interesting County Museum, housed in a recently restored workhouse. Letterkenny prides itself on its entertainment facilities, which include plenty of typically Irish bars, several of which offer Irish music; numerous nightclubs, including one of the largest in Ireland; and a good cinema centre. The town holds an International Folk Festival every August.

St. Columba has a connection of a sort with the area round Letterkenny, as with so many other places in Donegal. It was here that he eventually killed the man-eating monster called Swilly (or *Suileach*, in Irish), although the saint still had to contend with the various pieces into which he had cut the monster, all of which continued to attack him.

Around Donegal's Dramatic Coast

Broad Lough Swilly is a sea lough, dividing the Inishowen Peninsula, Donegal's most northerly and most easterly point, from the Fanad peninsula to the west. Inishowen is the largest of Donegal's peninsulas, though it is not so large that a leisurely tour round it by car cannot be fitted into a day. There are, however, many places which deserve a closer look rather than a cursory glance from a passing car.

There is Malin Head, for instance, at the peninsula's northern tip. Who, having listened to all those radio shipping forecasts, with their romantic-sounding names, could drive past this, Ireland's most northerly point, without stopping to look out over the Atlantic, perhaps even to glimpse a fishing boat pushing out to sea from one of the numerous villages and ports round the coast? The tower on the cliff here was originally built in 1805 by the British Admiralty to monitor shipping and was later used as a signal tower by Lloyd's of London.

In great contrast to Malin Head and its tower is Donegal's most ancient monument, the circular stone fort, Grianan of Aileach, at the southern end

of the peninsula 10km (6 miles) west of Letterkenny. The Grianán of Aileach dates back to the fifth century B.C. when it was probably a pagan temple. Later, it became a Christian site and St. Patrick is said to have baptized the founder of the O'Neill dynasty here in 450.

The northern coast of Donegal stretches westwards in a series of headlands, among the most scenic of which is Horn Head, rising 180m (600 ft) straight out of the Atlantic and offering a haven to a rich variety of birdlife. The coast turns south at Bloody Foreland, so-called because the rocks of the headland glow ruby-red at sunset. Out to sea between Horn Head and Bloody Foreland is Tory Island, separated from the northwest corner of Donegal by the turbulent Tory Channel and accessible by boat from Gortahork, daily in summer and weather permitting in winter.

Tory Island has its place in Celtic mythology as the home of Balor of the Evil Eye; even today, the islanders maintain a Celtic tradition by

speaking Gaelic and having their own monarch. They have also developed in recent years their own school of primitive artists, inspired by a local man, James Dixon, who felt that he could do better work than the visiting English painter, Derek Hill (of Glebe House), and they have recently opened a gallery on the island to show their work.

This northern part of Donegal, centred on Gortahork, but stretching from Fanad Head round the west coast down to the 601-metre (1,972-foot) Slieve League, whose south face rises sheer out of the sea on the northern shore of Donegal Bay, is one of Ireland's regions of *Gaeltacht*. At its southern extremity the area of *Gaeltacht* overlaps with modern tourism, for Donegal Bay is a holiday mecca for thousands of people every summer, and Bundoran, on the bay's southern shore, is one of Ireland's liveliest seaside resorts, full of amusement arcades, aquaworlds, souvenir shops and bright lights. Great fun in itself, Bundoran is so different from the country north of Donegal Bay in a world of its own.

Lying almost in the shadow of Slieve League is the village of Glencolumbkille (the 'Glen of Saint Colmcille') and its nearby Folk Village Museum, a recreation of Donegal rural life through the ages. Glencolumbkille's remote, rugged setting at the head of Glen Bay seems the perfect place to have built a retreat for prayer and contemplation and one can see why St. Columba should have chosen it. It is still a place of pilgrimage, and pilgrims make a penitential walk round the glen in the early hours of the morning of 9 June, the saint's feast day, stopping to pray at Stations of the Cross marked by boulders, cairns and even pagan standing stones.

More taxing by far than this mid-summer pilgrimage is Donegal's other famous religious event, at Station Island in Lough Derg, southeast of Donegal town, where the desire to partake in an extremely rigorous three-day retreat has attracted pilgrims since at least the 12th century.

In County Leitrim

Both Sligo and Leitrim stretch to the southern shores of Donegal Bay, though their hold on it is rather more tenuous than Donegal's. There is a feeling that, once you have travelled down the narrow strip that connects Donegal to the rest of the Republic, you have come to a quieter, more unobtrusive part of the country. Indeed, if you stick to the coast road from Bundoran, it is possible to be through Leitrim and into Sligo almost without noticing.

Leitrim's two-mile coastline has only one town, Tullaghan, one of Ireland's less exciting resorts, though the Drowes and Duff rivers which flow into the sea on either side of the village offer excellent salmon fishing. The 1,000-year-old high cross which stands on a mound nearby was not always there: it was found in the sea in the 18th century, having probably come from a monastery which once stood on the shore near the mouth of the Drowes.

Travel a little way inland from Leitrim's coast, and you are in a more interesting landscape, where deep valleys, such as Glencar and Glenade, cutting through the surprisingly rugged mountains, offer fine walking and its rivers attract fishermen eager to do battle with salmon and other freshwater fish. Centuries ago, the battles were far bloodier, involving the warriors of numerous local chiefs.

Dromahair, almost on the border with Sligo near Lough Gill, first found a place in history in the fifth century as the home of St. Patrick for 17 years, the saint founding a church, a monastery and a nunnery in this quiet place on the River Bonet. Seven centuries later, Dromahair, by now a seat of the powerful O'Rourke family, was again thrust into the forefront of Irish history when Dervorgilla, wife of Tiernan O'Rourke, Prince of Breifne, was abducted by Dermot MacMurrough, King of Leinster. Eventually, the abduction cost MacMurrough his throne, and he appealed to Henry II of England for help in getting it back. Thus, the Anglo-Normans marched into Irish history.

Much of the rest of Leitrim is dominated by loughs and rivers. The Shannon, flowing through spectacular Lough Allen, which virtually divides the county in two, is just one of many rivers and waterways, including the Ballinamore-Ballyconnell Canal, which make south Leitrim a fisherman's paradise. Here, the high plateau, falling away to the hillocks of the drumlin country round Mohill, is good country for ramblers and walkers on land and for cruising holidaymakers on water.

One of the northwest's most popular centres for coarse fishing and for cruising holidays is Leitrim's county town, Carrick-on-Shannon, set on a broad stretch of the Shannon below Lough Key. Apart from its fine lock and other waterworks, built early in the19th century when Carrick was an important town on Ireland's water transport system, the small town's main point of interest is its possession of Ireland's smallest church, the Costello Memorial Chapel. This tiny place, crammed between two buildings, was built in 1877 by a local merchant, Edward Costello, as a memorial and burial place for his young wife, Josephine. Both the Costellos now lie buried in lead coffins protected by thick slabs of glass, in the chapel.

The River Drowes is a gently flowing dividing line between the counties of Donegal and Leitrim near Bundoran. Beyond is the Dartry mountain range.

In the Land of William Butler Yeats

ABOVE
William Butler Yeats,
photographed when he was
about 40.

ABOVE RIGHT
Yeats' grave in the Protestant churchyard at
Drumcliff in Co. Sligo. The poet wrote his own
epitaph, carved on the headstone of his grave:

'Cast a cold eye
On life, on death.
Horseman, pass by!'

Geologists tell us that much of County Sligo was carved out by Ice-Age glaciers, leaving in the south of the county the lovely valleys and glittering lakes which makes this landscape one of the finest in Connaught. Further north, the country, marked by more lakes but dominated by limestone outcrops, of which Ben Bulben is the most striking, has been made even lovelier in the minds of men by the poetry of William Butler Yeats.

County Sligo is not Yeats' home county: he was born in Dublin, was educated there and in London, and spent half his life outside Ireland. But his deep love of Irish culture and the country of the northwest, immortalized in some of his finest poetry, forever links him with County Sligo.

Having spent many of the happiest days of his childhood there, he recalled, years later, times spent at the pretty resort of Rosses Point at the entrance to Sligo Bay, at Glencar Lough, or at Lough Gill and its tiny Isle of Innisfree, where 'midnight's all a glimmer, and noon a purple glow', to quote one of his best-known poems, *The Lake Isle of Innisfree*. Yeats' family had many connections with the town of Sligo, the largest in the northwest after Derry, and although Yeats himself owned a home in County Galway, near his friend Lady Gregory's home at Coole Park, it was the village of Drumcliff, near Sligo, that Yeats chose as his burial place, 'under bare Ben Bulben's head'.

Yeats died in the south of France in 1939 and it was not until 1948 that his body was brought back to Ireland, to be buried in the Protestant churchyard in Drumcliff. Today, Drumcliff is one of the highlights of regularly planned tours of 'Yeats Country', which attract many thousands of visitors to Sligo.

While Yeats may have become one of Sligo's greatest tourist attractions, he is not its only one. Yeats loved Sligo as much for its splendid culture, packed full of historical incident and myth, as for the beauty of its countryside, and these same things continue to attract people today.

For those interested in Ireland's ancient past, County Sligo holds a special fascination. At the Carrowmore Megalithic Cemetery, south of Sligo,

can be seen tombs at least 700 years older than the famous ones at Newgrange in County Meath. Carrowmore is the second-largest megalithic tomb site in Europe, with only Carnac in France exceeding it in size. Then there are the passage tombs at Carrowkeel, high in the Bricklieve Mountains in the south of the county. Here, passage graves, set in limestone cairns, date from 2500-2000 B.C. One of the roofed tombs, cruciform-shaped Cairn K, can be entered, a spine-tingling step into the distant past.

For those whose interest is more recent history, an evocative trip can be made to the island of Innishmurray, 6km (4 miles) off Sligo's northern coast, where Saint Molaise founded a monastery in the sixth century. The Vikings

destroyed much of it, but there are still three churches to be seen and a beehive hut which was once a school. About 50 stone memorials are scattered over the island, at which pilgrims performed the Stations of the Cross until as recently as 1948.

A trip of a different kind is the hike many people make up the southeast flank of Knocknarea, the 'Hill of the Kings', west of Sligo town. At the hill's summit is a 5,000-year-old passage grave and tomb, popularly believed to be the burial place of the legendary Maeve, Queen of Connaught, one of the great characters of Celtic mythology.

Tranquil Lough Gill, with the Dartry Mountains beyond, was a favourite place for the poet. Would he have heard the silvery sound of the bell from the Dominican Abbey in Sligo which is said to lie at the bottom of the lake? Only those without sin, says a legend associated with the lake, can hear it.

Chapter Eight
Northern Ireland –
Antrim, Armagh, Down, Fermanagh, Derry and Tyrone

Six of the nine counties of the ancient province of Ulster became part of the United Kingdom, as the Province of Northern Ireland, under the Anglo-Irish Treaty of 1921. Of the six counties, Armagh is the smallest and Tyrone the least populated; Antrim boasts the Province's main tourist attractions, including the Giant's Causeway and the lovely Glens of Antrim while Fermanagh, the only one of the six not to claim a share of vast Lough Neagh's shoreline, is the lake district of Ireland, with a third of its area under stretches of water which include the lovely Upper Lough Erne and Lower Lough Erne. Both County Derry and County Down are steeped in history and rich in fine scenery.

Today, despite 30 years of the 'Troubles', as the Irish refer with remarkable coolness and restraint to the hideous carnage of bombings and shootings that has polarized society north of the Border, life in the six counties is good and the country itself remains as lovely and as accessible as it has always been.

Recent co-operation between the Province and the Republic in restoring the Ballinamore-Ballyconnell Canal, linking the River Shannon with the lakes and rivers of Fermanagh has helped make the lovely country around the canal and river system accessible to many more people, with holidaymakers, on pleasure boats and cruisers, able to enjoy much more of the serene beauty which surrounds them.

The peace process of recent years has also brought a new feeling of optimism to the people of Northern Ireland. It is an optimism well expressed in the province's considerable programme of rebuilding, with many attractive modern buildings going up on bombed and derelict sites.

Among the finest of these, and perhaps one which best expresses the new spirit abroad in Northern Ireland, is Belfast's Waterfront Hall, described as 'a fresh, Modernist take on the Albert Hall', which was opened early in 1997. This splendid concert hall, with its glittering, curved glass frontage, stands on the bank of the River Lagan in a part of the city where the skyline has been dominated for many years by the great cranes of the Harland and Wolff Shipyard. Near the Waterfront Hall, there is a hotel (one of an international chain), numerous office buildings, new shops, multi-storey car parks – Belfast, Northern Ireland's administrative centre and largest city, is reaching towards the Millennium as vigorously as the Republic's capital, Dublin.

Belfast Today

There was a time, in the 19th century, when Belfast's growth far outstripped that of Dublin, for the great industrial expansion of Victorian England spread across the Irish Sea to Belfast rather than to Dublin, and Belfast became one of the world's major engineering and shipbuilding centres as well as an important manufacturer of

rope and linen, the latter industry having been founded in the 17th century by French Huguenots.

There are many signs of Belfast's 19th-century prosperity still to be seen in the city today, from the imposing and splendidly domed City Hall in Donegall Square and the neo-Romanesque St. Anne's Anglican Cathedral in Donegall Street to the Grand Opera House, nicknamed by Belfast 'the eastern palace' on account of its eastern appearance with the onion domes atop its façade. Belfast's well-known Linen Hall Library, also in Donegall Square, no longer has any connection with Northern Ireland's important linen weaving industry. The White Linen Hall in which it is housed was established as a library in 1788 and now has the best collection in existence of early books printed in Belfast. It is here that you can study the huge number of works on political life in Northern Ireland published since 1966.

A gentle 15-minute stroll from Donegall Square, the hub of Belfast from which most of the city's main streets radiate, leads to another grand example of 19th-century architecture, still fulfilling an important role as this century draws to a close. This is the main building of Queen's University, Northern Ireland's most prestigious seat of learning and attracting students from many parts of the world.

Opposite the Grand Opera House in Great Victoria Street is an unforgettable Victorian 'gin palace', The Crown Liquor Saloon, a pub exuberantly decorated with tiles and stained glass, carved oak and gaslights. The Saloon belongs to the National Trust, a body which has many of the finest buildings and most precious tracts of countryside in Northern Ireland within its careful guardianship. The National Trust, in preserving these different aspects of Northern Ireland's heritage, is working along appropriate lines, for throughout Northern Ireland the many intertwining strands of the province's history can be best understood against the background of its fine scenery.

OPPOSITE
Co. Fermanagh waterscape: a view from the Cliffs of Magho across Lower Lough Erne.

ABOVE
The dome of Belfast's City Hall dominates this view of the centre of the city. Completed in 1906 in a grand Renaissance style intended to emphasize Belfast's industrial prosperity, the City Hall housed the first meeting of the Northern Ireland parliament in 1921.

TOP LEFT
A statue of Lord Carson of Duncairn who, as Sir Edward Carson, was the main architect of the Province of Northern Ireland, stands in front of Stormont, former home of the Northern Ireland parliament and now government offices.

TOP RIGHT
Belfast's Waterfront Hall is a splendid addition to the cultural life of the Province.

Where History and Countryside Merge

Visit Navan Fort in the heart of quietly rural County Armagh, for instance, and explore the great circular enclosure with its man-made central mound, and you are transported back to the mists of Celtic myth and ancient Irish history. This place, once called Emain Macha, was the capital from where Celtic kings and queens ruled ancient Ulster. In use as long ago as 2000 B.C., the site was most actively occupied in the century before Christ. The great folk hero, Cúchulainn, the Hound of Ulster, is associated with the place, as are the mythical Red Branch Knights.

Cuchulainn's exploits, celebrated in myth and legend, also emphasize the separation in history of Ulster from the other provinces of Ireland: there has always been a border of sorts between the people of Ulster and those of the other ancient provinces of Ireland.

Emain Macha was founded by Queen Macha, celebrated in mythology as the Celtic war-fertility goddess, who also gave her name to Armagh (*Ard Mhacha* means 'Macha's Height'), the county town and one of Ireland's oldest cities just two miles (or a quick cycle ride in this fine cycling country) to the east of Navan Fort. This small, quietly handsome town, is at the heart of Irish Christianity, for St. Patrick founded two churches here in the fifth century. Today, Armagh is the ecclesiastical capital of Catholic Ireland, with its heart in St. Patrick's Cathedral. The city is also the seat of the Anglican Primacy in Ireland,

centred on the Church of Ireland cathedral, built on the site of St. Patrick's second church.

St. Patrick himself first landed in Ireland as a missionary at Strangford Lough on the coast of County Down in A.D. 432. He built his first church at nearby Saul, sailing up the little River Slaney from the lough. There is a memorial chapel and Celtic-style round tower there now, built in the 1930s to commemorate Ireland's most ancient ecclesiastical site. St. Patrick's church is long gone, of course, as is the monastery built by St. Malachy in the 12th century.

St. Patrick's remains are in Downpatrick, the capital of County Down, probably buried under the cathedral, an early 19th-century building on a site which had known many churches over the centuries. Built where several river valleys converge, Downpatrick, not surprisingly, endured many destructive invasions over the centuries, but it also, during and after the period of the Jacobite plantations, attracted many settlers.

Down has witnessed the mingling of political and religious history which has marked Irish life for centuries. After St. Patrick, Christianity spread rapidly through Ulster, as it did through the rest of Ireland. The Anglo-Normans who, unlike the Vikings, remained to settle in the lands they had invaded, managed to maintain an uneasy peace with the Irish chieftains who ruled alongside them. Elizabeth I, fearful that her realm would be invaded by Spain via the back door of Ireland, ended this relatively comfortable co-existence and began the system of sending Protestants from England (especially London), and from Scotland to set up plantations of loyal citizens in Ireland. Her successor, James VI and I of Scotland, continued the policy even more strenuously which resulted in the infamous 'Flight of the Earls', and the establishment of a Protestant-based rule from which Irish Catholics were excluded.

Among the many towns of Northern Ireland to have been given their present style and shape by this system of plantation are Fermanagh's county town of Enniskillen, set in a narrow spit of land between Upper and Lower Lough Erne and concentrated round the 15th-century Enniskillen Castle, and Derry's Coleraine, now a quiet market town and site of the modern campus of the University of Ulster.

County Derry was particularly heavily planted by Protestant settlers in the 17th century, many of them sent over by City of London companies, which is why the old city of Derry came to be renamed Londonderry. Derry has grown up round a monastery founded by St. Columba in the sixth century and when the old city was destroyed by fire it was rebuilt by a consortium of City of London companies in the early 17th century. Thus, Derry, too, is a plantation town, which achieved the most celebrated moment in its history when it withstood a long siege in 1689 by the army of the Catholic James II, in his attempt to win back his lost throne. Today, Derry is the second most important city in Northern Ireland and has been going through a process of rejuvenation in recent years.

ABOVE
The corbelled turrets of Enniskillen Castle rise above the waterway which links Upper and Lower Lough Erne. Much of the small town of Enniskillen is built on an island in the waterway.

OPPOSITE TOP
Gazing at the world from the distant past, this Celtic head in Armagh Cathedral dates from the Iron Age.

OPPOSITE BELOW
Armagh has two cathedrals named after Saint Patrick: this is the Church of Ireland's St. Patrick's Cathedral, seat of the Protestant Archbishop of Armagh.

Northern Ireland's Glorious Coastline

Derry, standing on the River Foyle which flows into Lough Foyle and onwards into the Atlantic Ocean, had a special place in the hearts of many of the people of Ulster in the 19th century, for hundreds of families fleeing famine departed for North America from here. Their last sight of Ireland would have taken in the city, the lough and the coastline, indented and broken by rivers and sea loughs, gradually disappearing below the horizon.

Many of Northern Ireland's greatest scenic attractions are to be found along its coast, ranging from the golden sands of Benone Strand, Ireland's longest beach at the tip of Lough Foyle, right round to the Mourne coast, where County Down's beautiful Mountains of Mourne, celebrated in poetry and song, reach down to the sea.

In between, there is something for everyone. Most spectacular on the northern coast is, of

magnificent in County Antrim where the Glens of Antrim stretch towards the coast, three of them converging near Cushendall, also boasts some of the Province's most historic buildings. Two of the finest are the superbly preserved Carrickfergus Castle, whose massive keep dominates the harbour at Carrickfergus, on the north shore of Belfast Lough and, further south on the Ards Peninsula overlooking Strangford Lough in County Down, Mount Stewart House.

The latter, dating mostly from the 19th century, has a wonderfully grand interior but its great attraction are the superb gardens in which the house is set. Created by Edith, Lady Londonderry in the 1920s, the gardens of Mount Stewart House are now rated among the finest in the United Kingdom. The house, once the home of the powerful Londonderry family, whose most famous scion was the British Foreign Secretary of the early 19th century, Lord Castlereagh, is now the jewel in the crown of the National Trust in Northern Ireland. Among its finest attractions are Stubbs' celebrated painting of the racehorse

Hambletonian, which hangs in the house, and the lovely Temple of the Winds, built as a banqueting pavilion in 1785, in the grounds.

Strangford Lough, largest of the sea loughs of Northern Ireland's east and south coasts, is an area of considerable beauty with many places of interest. These include several castles clustered around its seaward end; the village of Saul, where St. Patrick is believed to have established his first church in Ireland; and, near its western shore, the fascinating pre-Norman monastic site of Nendrum on Mahee Island, one of nearly 120 islands in the lough.

Strangford Lough comprises one of Europe's richest maritime habitats. Visit the lough in early summer and you could see hundreds of common seals inhabiting the rocks and low reefs and, around the Narrows – the entrance to the lough – even a basking shark gliding through the water. There are giant skate in the deep waters and great shoals of herring fry, too. The lough's prolific marine life naturally attracts great numbers and varieties of birds, with many kinds of migrating birds appearing on the lough in the early autumn.

course, the Giant's Causeway, Ireland's only World Heritage Site. The estimated 37,000 basalt columns, most of them hexagonal in shape, which compose it, reach out from the cliffs of Antrim into the sea, pointing towards Scotland. So imposing is it that it is little wonder that the Giant's Causeway figures as greatly in the myths and legends of Ireland as in the textbooks of geologists.

Further east are other points of interest, including the alarming Carrick-a-Rede Rope Bridge, slung 25m (80 ft) above the sea near Ballintoy and much visited by tourists, and the market town of Ballycastle, whose famous Ould Lammas Fair still operates under a charter first granted in the 15th century. A 50-minute boat ride out to sea from Ballycastle and one arrives at Rathlin Island, called Raghery locally, where Bull Point at its western tip is home to tens of thousands of seabirds, including puffins, kittiwakes and razorbills.

Northern Ireland's east coast, at its most

TOP LEFT
Mussenden Temple, perched on the cliff edge at Downhill near Portstewart in Co. Derry is all that is left of the grand house the eccentric Bishop Hervey, who was also Earl of Bristol, built for himself in the mid-18th century.

OPPOSITE BELOW
Walking in the steps of Finn MacCool, this dog is surrounded by some of the 37,000 basalt columns

which make up the Giant's Causeway in Co. Antrim. Geologists tell us that the columns are the result, not of Finn MacCool's legendary activities, but of an underground volcanic eruption some 60 million years ago.

ABOVE
Intrepid walkers cross the Carrick-a-Rede rope bridge, slung between cliffs on the Co. Antrim coast near Ballintoy.

The Province's Inland Glories

Northern Ireland's coastline ends in the south on the shore of another great sea lough, Carlingford Lough. This, like others which indent the coast, leads naturally into the heart of the province. Though primarily agricultural, with rolling green hills stretching as far as the eye can see, Northern Ireland is dominated, in fact, by some splendid stretches of water and, in its northwest corner, by a superb range of hills bisected by gloriously beautiful glens.

There are nine Glens of Antrim, carved by rivers cutting through the high plateaus of the Antrim Mountains. Left 'unplanted' by the English and Scots in the 17th century, the Glens were for centuries wild and remote areas where the Gaelic language persisted for longer than anywhere else in Northern Ireland. Today, they are easily accessible from Antrim's fine coast road, allowing thousands of visitors every year to enjoy the beauty of the scenery, much of the finest of which is enclosed within the Glenariff Forest Park. Glenariff, the best-known of the glens, was described by the novelist Thackeray as 'Switzerland in miniature', a description which still holds good. Glenariff village (also called Waterfoot) hosts a festival of Irish music every July.

The most prominent village in the Glens is Cushendall, the 'Capital of the Glens', which sits below Glenballyemon, its streets creeping up the sides of the glen. Its most noticeable landmark is the Curfew Tower, built in 1809 as a prison for 'riotous persons'. For places of deeper historic significance, however, one should go beyond Cushendall into Glenaan, where Ossian's Grave, a Neolithic court tomb named after Finn MacCool's son, lies beside a steep path up Tievebulliagh mountain; or north a mile or so out of the village to Tiveragh where an ancient mound, the Fairy Hill, is said to be a place frequented by the 'wee folk'; then on to Layde Old Church, founded by the Franciscans and an important burial place of the MacDonnell clan.

While nine rivers carved the Glens of Antrim, it took the waters of six rivers, including the Province's longest, the Bann, converging in the heart of the Province, to create Lough Neagh, the largest inland lake in the British Isles. At least, that's the geologists' story. Irish legend has it that the lake was created when Finn MacCool, picking up a piece of turf one day, hurled it into the Irish Sea, thereby leaving a large hole and creating the Isle of Man at the same time.

Since much of Lough Neagh is bordered by sedgy marshland, there are few roads along its banks and it has not become a great centre for watersports, though there is plenty of excellent fishing along the rivers which flow into it. The lough is most famous, in fact, for its eels, on which a thriving industry is based, with Toome, on the north shore, having Europe's largest eel fishery.

Lough Neagh's most attractive recreational area is at its southern end. Oxford Island – really a peninsula – is home to an important nature reserve and bird-watching site. Further west, Peatlands Park is another excellent nature reserve with an informative visitors' centre. Coney Island, near the mouth of the Blackwater and one of the few islands in Lough Neagh, belongs to the National Trust. Once a retreat for St. Patrick, the island is mainly visited today for its varied and abundant birdlife.

Travel further south and west through the Province, and you come to a very different kind of lake scenery. Lower Lough Erne, a stretch of water covering much of the northern part of County Fermanagh and stretching, at its western edge, to within just a few miles of the Atlantic Ocean, has 97 islands scattered across it. One of the most important of these is Devenish Island,

5km (3 miles) from Enniskillen at the southeastern end of the Lough. Saint Molaise founded a monastery on the island in the sixth century which remained an important religious centre for a hundred years. Also well worth a visit are Boa Island, with strange pre-Christian stone figures in Caldragh cemetery, and White Island, where extraordinary stone figures were set into the wall of an old monastery centuries ago.

Because this is a historically rich part of Ireland, a tour round Lower Lough Erne, taking in Enniskillen in the east and Belleek in the west, offers a splendid collection of historic and natural sites of interest. There are castles, such as the fortified plantation house, Tully Castle, on the southern shore of the lough, remote Monea Castle, a well-preserved plantation castle, and Enniskillen's famous castle, dating back to the 15th century and now a heritage centre and home to the Inniskilling Regimental Museum. There is a forest park, a country park and the Lough Navar Scenic Route, a forest drive which leads to a superb viewpoint on the Cliffs of Magho, on Lower Lough Erne's southern shore. From up here, it is possible to see way over and beyond the waters of the lough to the Sperrin Mountains of Tyrone and the mountains of Sligo, Donegal and Leitrim.

Fermanagh's second largest lake is Upper Lough Erne, also dotted with islands and islets and surrounded by moorland country broken into a patchwork of fields, cut by rivers and smaller lakes and marked by conifer plantations. The lovely River Erne, flowing north from Cavan and creating Upper Lough Erne as it does so, is a link with the Republic.

OPPOSITE TOP
The pretty little fishing village of Strangford stretches along the southern shore of Strangford Lough where it narrows before reaching the sea. The Vikings, noting the strong tidal currents here, gave the place its name: 'Strong fjord'.

OPPOSITE BELOW
This two-faced Janus figure stands in Caldragh churchyard on Boa Island, at the northern end of Lough Erne. There is nothing quite like this extraordinary 2,000-year-old sculpture to be found anywhere else in Ireland.

ABOVE
Only the ruins remain of Tully Castle, near Belleek in Co. Fermanagh, built for a planter's family from Scotland early in the 17th century and destroyed and abandoned in 1641. Today, they provide a fine backdrop for carefully tended gardens in the bawn.

LEFT
The fine Palladian-style Florence Court in Co. Fermanagh is a beautifully maintained National Trust property. Built in the 18th century by the Cole family, descendants of the planters of nearby Enniskillen, the house is now popular with tourists and walkers.

Index